*Thought and W*

There is an important family of semantic notions that we apply to thoughts and to the conceptual constituents of thoughts – as when we say that the thought that the universe is expanding is true. *Thought and World* presents a theory of the content of such notions. The theory is largely deflationary in spirit, in the sense that it represents a broad range of semantic notions – including the concept of truth – as being entirely free from substantive metaphysical and empirical presuppositions. At the same time, however, it takes seriously and seeks to explain the intuition that there is a metaphysically or empirically "deep" relation (a relation of mirroring or semantic correspondence) linking thoughts to reality. Thus, the theory represents a kind of compromise between deflationism and the correspondence theory of truth.

This book will appeal to students and professionals interested in the philosophy of logic and philosophy of language.

Christopher S. Hill is Professor of Philosophy at the University of Arkansas, Fayetteville.

CAMBRIDGE STUDIES IN PHILOSOPHY

*General editor*    ERNEST SOSA    (Brown University)

*Advisory editors:*
JONATHAN DANCY    (University of Reading)
JOHN HALDANE    (University of St. Andrews)
GILBERT HARMAN    (Princeton University)
FRANK JACKSON    (Australian National University)
WILLIAM G. LYCAN    (University of North Carolina at Chapel Hill)
SYDNEY SHOEMAKER    (Cornell University)
JUDITH J. THOMSON    (Massachusetts Institute of Technology)

RECENT TITLES:

BARRY MAUND    *Colours*
MICHAEL DEVITT    *Coming to Our Senses*
MICHAEL ZIMMERMAN    *The Concept of Moral Obligation*
MICHAEL STOCKER with ELIZABETH HEGEMAN    *Valuing Emotions*
SYDNEY SHOEMAKER    *The First-Person Perspective and Other Essays*
NORTON NELKIN    *Consciousness and the Origins of Thought*
MARK LANCE and JOHN O'LEARY HAWTHORNE    *The Grammar of Meaning*
D.M. ARMSTRONG    *A World of States of Affairs*
PIERRE JACOB    *What Minds Can Do*
ANDRE GALLOIS    *The World Without the Mind Within*
FRED FELDMAN    *Utilitarianism, Hedonism, and Desert*
LAURENCE BONJOUR    *In Defense of Pure Reason*
DAVID LEWIS    *Papers in Philosophical Logic*
WAYNE DAVIS    *Implicature*
DAVID COCKBURN    *Other Times*
DAVID LEWIS    *Papers on Metaphysics and Epistemology*
RAYMOND MARTIN    *Self-Concern*
ANNETTE BARNES    *Seeing Through Self-Deception*
MICHAEL BRATMAN    *Faces of Intention*
AMIE THOMASSON    *Fiction and Metaphysics*
DAVID LEWIS    *Papers on Ethics and Social Philosophy*
FRED DRETSKE    *Perception, Knowledge and Belief*
LYNNE RUDDER BAKER    *Persons and Bodies*
JOHN GRECO    *Putting Skeptics in Their Place*
DERK PEREBOOM    *Living Without Free Will*
BRIAN ELLIS    *Scientific Essentialism*
JULIA DRIVER    *Uneasy Virtue*
RICHARD FOLEY    *Intellectual Trust in Oneself and Others*

# Thought and World

## An Austere Portrayal of Truth, Reference, and Semantic Correspondence

CHRISTOPHER S. HILL

CAMBRIDGE
UNIVERSITY PRESS

PUBLISHED BY THE PRESS SYNDICATE OF THE UNIVERSITY OF CAMBRIDGE
The Pitt Building, Trumpington Street, Cambridge, United Kingdom

CAMBRIDGE UNIVERSITY PRESS
The Edinburgh Building, Cambridge CB2 2RU, UK
40 West 20th Street, New York, NY 10011-4211, USA
477 Williamstown Road, Port Melbourne, VIC 3207, Australia
Ruiz de Alarcón 13, 28014 Madrid, Spain
Dock House, The Waterfront, Cape Town 8001, South Africa

http://www.cambridge.org

First published 2002

Printed in the United Kingdom at the University Press, Cambridge

*Typeface* Bembo 10.5/13 pt.    *System* LATEX $2_\varepsilon$  [TB]

*A catalog record for this book is available from the British Library.*

*Library of Congress Cataloging in Publication Data available*

ISBN 0 521 81484 7 hardback
ISBN 0 521 89243 0 paperback

*For my children*
*Katrina Hill*
*Jonathan Hill*

# Contents

# Acknowledgments

My primary philosophical debt is to Anil Gupta. He has been outstandingly generous with his time and energy, placing his remarkable talents at my disposal whenever I have needed them. I have also benefited significantly from interactions with Barbara Abbott, Bradley Armour-Garb, Gordon Beavers, Anthony Brueckner, Robert Cummins, Marian David, Sandra Edwards, Hartry Field, Ivan Fox, Marcus Giaquinto, Allan Gibbard, Delia Graff, Jane Heal, Joel Katzav, Richard Lee, Vann McGee, Brian McLaughlin, Hugh Mellor, Edward Minar, Christopher Peacocke, Nathan Salmon, Thomas Senor, T. J. Smiley, Ernest Sosa, Paul Vincent Spade, James Spellman, Jamie Tappenden, and Timothy Williamson.

Various portions of the book have served as the bases for colloquium talks at the University of Sheffield, the University of Cambridge, Rutgers University, St. Louis University, and the London School of Economics. The discussions on those occasions were both stimulating and illuminating. In addition, I have profited from the discussion following a talk at a meeting of the American Philosophical Association.

Anil Gupta and Ted Warfield gave me extensive comments on the penultimate version of the manuscript. Their advice has enabled me to avoid many sins, both of omission and commission. I have also been helped considerably by the comments of an anonymous referee for Cambridge University Press.

My chief personal debts are of course to my family and friends, but I must also acknowledge the very considerable contributions to my welfare that have been made by my bicycle and by the flora and fauna of Kingston, Arkansas.

Chapters 2 and 3 contain excerpts from two of my papers that appeared in *Philosophical Studies* (1999, 96/1, pp. 87–121; 2001, 104/3, pp. 291–321). I wish to thank Kluwer Academic Publishers for their kind permission to reprint this material, and also Stewart Cohen, the editor of *Philosophical Studies*, for his continuing support for my work.

Finally, I gratefully acknowledge financial support from the University of Arkansas.

# 1

# *Introduction*

Pilate said to him, "So you are a king?" Jesus answered, "You say that I am a king. For this I was born, and for this I have come into the world, to bear witness to the truth. Everyone who is of the truth hears my voice." Pilate said to him, "What is truth?"

*(John* 19, 37–38[1])

I

When one has a belief, one is thereby related to a *proposition*. Thus, for example, if one believes that the universe is expanding, one stands in a certain psychological relation, the relation of believing, to the proposition that the universe is expanding. One is also related to this proposition if one fears that the universe is expanding or one hopes that the universe is expanding. In general, propositions are the objects to which we are related by the family of psychological relations that includes believing, fearing, hoping, desiring, intending, and considering.

We often claim that a proposition is *true*. Thus, we are all prepared to say that the proposition that snow is white is true. I will be concerned in this work to explain what we have in mind when we make such claims. That is to say, I will be concerned to analyze the concept of *propositional truth*. In addition, I will be concerned to adjudicate the various disputes about this concept that have traditionally divided philosophers.

To the extent that these efforts are successful, they will, I believe, illuminate the entire fabric of our thought and talk about truth. Thus, as I see it, while there are concepts of truth other than the concept of propositional truth, the latter concept is the most fundamental one, and is in fact the source of the content and value of the others. If this view is correct, a theory that contributes to our understanding of the concept of propositional truth will also contribute to our understanding of its fellows.

To elaborate: Apart from the concept of propositional truth, the concepts of truth with which we are most concerned are the concepts of *sentential truth* and *doxastic truth*. These are, respectively, the notions that figure in (1) and (2):

(1) The sentence "Snow is white" is true in English.
(2) The belief that snow is white is true.

Now it is extremely plausible that these two concepts can be explained reductively in terms of the concept of propositional truth. To see that this holds in the case of sentential truth, observe that it is extremely plausible to say that speakers use sentences to express propositions – to say, for example, that speakers of English use the sentence "Snow is white" to express the proposition that snow is white. Assuming that this appealing view is correct, it is natural to explain sentential truth by saying that a sentence is true if the proposition that it is used to express is true. To see that the notion of doxastic truth can be reductively explained as well, observe that beliefs are naturally understood as "involving" propositions, that is, as being relational properties that have propositions as constituents, in the way that the relational property *north of Boston* has Boston as a constituent. It follows from this view that it is possible to explain the truth of beliefs by saying that a belief counts as true if the proposition that is involved in the belief is true.

It appears, then, that the concept of propositional truth is more basic than the concepts of sentential and doxastic truth. It follows that if our investigation of the former concept meets with success, it will enhance our understanding of the latter concepts.

The notion of a proposition will inevitably play a large role in the following reflections. In the early stages I will limit myself to two assumptions about the nature of propositions. To be specific, I will assume only that they have logical structures, and that concepts are their fundamental building blocks. Eventually, in Chapter 5, I will supplement these assumptions about propositions with a few assumptions about the nature of concepts. In combination with the claim that concepts are the building blocks of propositions, the latter assumptions will provide the foundation for a metaphysical theory of propositions, telling us, among other things, how propositions are individuated.

The assumption that propositions have logical structure should be stressed. It is intended in a very strong sense – specifically, as claiming that it is appropriate to view propositions as having constituent structures that parallel the logical structures of sentences. It is meant to entail, for example, that it is appropriate to regard the proposition *Hannibal crossed the Alps and Caesar crossed the Rubicon* as a complex structure consisting of two simpler propositions and a logical concept (the concept of conjunction). It is also meant to entail that it is appropriate to think of each of the simpler propositions as having an internal logical organization, an organization that can be expressed by saying that the proposition consists of two nominal concepts and a predicative concept that plays the role of a transitive verb. Claims of this sort are not universally accepted; but they have considerable intuitive appeal, and they are defended in the literature by powerful arguments.[2]

It is common among philosophers to use "proposition" in the way that I am using it here – that is, as referring to the objects of propositional attitudes, and therefore, as referring to entities that have logical structures and are constructed from concepts. It must be acknowledged, however, that in addition to this primary sense, "proposition" has a secondary sense that is quite different. Thus, the term is sometimes used to refer to states of affairs, and therefore, to entities that are constructed from such extra-conceptual building blocks as substances, properties, and relations. With a view to avoiding the problems that might be occasioned by this ambiguity, I will frequently use the term "thought" in place of "proposition" in the present work. Thus, in these pages, "thought" is used as a term for the objects to which we are related by such attitudes as belief, desire, and intention.[3] Also, it carries a commitment to the assumption that the objects in question are logically structured, and to the assumption that they have concepts as their ultimate constituents. There are of course other ways of using "thought." As far as I can determine, however, the various meanings of "thought" are more similar to one another than the various meanings of "proposition." Accordingly, there will be less of a risk of confusion if I give preference to "thought" over "proposition" in formulating key principles and arguments.

II

The theory of truth that I will recommend is a version of the view that is known as *deflationism*. That is to say, it is a version of the view that truth is philosophically and empircally neutral, in the sense that its use carries no substantive philosophical or empirical commitments.

The simplest and clearest example of a deflationary theory is the account of truth that Paul Horwich has presented under the name *minimalism*. According to Horwich, the concept of propositional truth is defined by the totality of thoughts that have the following form:

(T) The thought that *p* is true if and only if *p*.

In other words, according to Horwich, the concept is defined by the totality of thoughts that have the same form as the following thought:

The thought that the Universe is expanding is true if and only if the Universe is expanding.

Horwich explains this doctrine by saying that a person's understanding of the concept of truth "consists in his disposition to accept, without evidence, any instantiation of the schema" (T).[4]

If minimalism is correct, then there is no particular set of concepts that one must acquire prior to acquiring the concept of truth, and it is possible to acquire the concept without learning any particular philosophical or empirical theory. To master the concept, it is sufficient to acquire the ability to recognize thoughts that have a certain *form*, and to learn that thoughts of that form are always to be accepted. It can be said, then, that minimalism represents the concept of truth as autonomous and presuppositionless. By the same token, it can be said that minimalism represents this concept as one that can be used without running any philosophical or empirical risks – that is, without being committed to any philosophical or empirical doctrines that could turn out to be wrong.[5]

Although there are important differences of detail, all versions of deflationism share with minimalism the optimistic message that the concept of truth is philosophically and empirically innocuous, and most agree that thoughts of form (T) are intimately related to the content of the concept. It follows that versions of deflationism tend to have a strong appeal. It is, after all, quite pleasing to be told that in this risk-filled world, there is one piece of equipment that can be used without fear of adverse philosophical or empirical consequences! Moreover, it is extremely plausible that thoughts of form (T) have a special status. We are strongly inclined to believe that acceptance of them is forced upon us by the content of the concept of truth, and that they are somehow deeply revelatory of that content.

In the twentieth century, deflationism was championed by a number of very able philosophers, including Ayer, Belnap, Camp, Field, Grover, Horwich, Leeds, Quine, Ramsey, and Strawson.[6] But there are anticipations in a number of earlier writers. Indeed, it is possible to read the very earliest pronouncements about truth in Western philosophy as being largely deflationary in spirit. Consider, for example, Aristotle's famous definition at *Metaphysics* Γ, 7, 10011[b], 26–8:

To say of what is that it is not, or of what is not that it is, is false, while to say of what is that it is, or of what is not that it is not, is true.[7]

This suggestive passage admits of a variety of interpretations, including some that are at odds with deflationism. But to my mind, the most natural interpretation is that Aristotle means to explain falsity and truth in terms of four schemas that are equivalent to the following:

(1) If it is not the case that $p$ and one says that $p$, then what one says is false.
(2) If it is the case that $p$ and one says that it is not the case that $p$, then what one says is false.
(3) If it is the case that $p$ and one says that $p$, then what one says is true.
(4) If it is not the case that $p$ and one says that it is not the case that $p$, then what one says is true.

Now contemporary deflationists frequently cite schemas of this sort in explaining their position. Indeed, reflection shows that schemas (3) and (4) are closely related to the schema that serves as the foundation of Horwich's theory of truth. It turns out, then, that there is a plausible way of interpreting Aristotle which represents him as anticipating Horwichian minimalism.[8,9]

The version of deflationism that I will propose is significantly different than Horwich's version, but it is nonetheless true that I am an ardent admirer of the latter view. I applaud the clarity and elegance of minimalism, and I believe that it goes a long way toward being materially adequate. Accordingly, in addition to advocating my own version of deflationism in the following pages, I will often be concerned to champion minimalism. Whenever possible, I will rely on arguments that are designed to promote both theories simultaneously. If this approach has the desired effect, then even if the reader is not moved by the arguments that are meant specifically to favor my preferred version of deflationism, he or she will still be left with positive feelings about the family of deflationary theories, and perhaps even with the sense that the deflationary approach represents our best hope of explaining truth.

Among the various alternatives to deflationary accounts of truth, the ones that have historically received the greatest attention are versions of the *correspondence theory* – that is, versions of the view that truth consists in some sort of representational or mirroring relationship between thoughts and the world.

The correspondence theory has had many distinguished advocates. The earliest in the West may have been Avicenna, who wrote in the *Metaphysics* that "truth is understood as . . . the disposition of speech or understanding that signifies the disposition in the external thing when it is equal to it."[10] Avicenna's pronouncement was cited with approval by William of Auvergne,[11] and Aquinas embraced a similar doctrine ("truth is the adaequation of intellect and thing").[12] As these examples suggest, it appears that medieval philosophers favored the form of the correspondence theory which asserts that truth consists in a relation between thought (or speech, or belief) and *objects* or *things* (as opposed to *facts* or *states of affairs*).[13] This form of the view has continued to attract a following. Thus Kant appears to have endorsed two versions of it, maintaining both that "truth consist in agreement of knowledge with the object," and that truth is "the conformity of our thoughts with the object."[14] And in the twentieth century, this *objectualist* form of the correspondence theory was given a new formulation by Alfred Tarski, and became quite popular in that guise.[15]

The *factualist* form of the correspondence theory seems to have made a later appearance in the philosophical literature than the objectualist form; indeed, as far as I have been able to determine, it did not receive much explicit attention until the twentieth century. As we will see, however, there are good reasons to think that it is the version of the correspondence theory that is most defensible, and also the form that is most deeply rooted in our conceptual scheme. Russell proposed a version of factualism in *The Problems of Philosophy*, maintaining that "a belief is true when there is a corresponding fact, and false when there is no corresponding fact."[16] Wittgenstein held a similar view, as did Moore.[17] Austin defended a factualist doctrine at mid-century,[18] and in more recent times, D. M. Armstrong has argued persuasively for the inevitability of factualism.[19]

Correspondence theorists have been moved by intuitions of two kinds. First, there are intuitions to the effect that there is a relation of representation or semantic correspondence that links thoughts (or sentences, or beliefs) to the world. And second, there are intuitions to the effect that this relation is somehow importantly linked to truth. In Chapter 3 I will argue that these intuitions have impressive credentials, and that it is necessary to treat them with respect.

It is unusual for deflationists to arrive at such conclusions, for one of the chief tenets of standard forms of deflationism is that truth can be grasped independently of understanding of what it is for a thought (or a sentence, or a belief) to correspond to reality. I will maintain, however, that it is possible to honor the intuitions that appear to favor the correspondence theory without abandoning the core commitments of deflationism. Thus, I will argue that the relation of semantic correspondence is significantly less problematic than deflationists have recognized. It is, I will maintain, a reasonably straightforward relation, one that can be fully characterized in terms of notions that are familiar and well motivated. Furthermore, while acknowledging that there are significant a priori connections between the concept of correspondence and the concept of truth, I will argue that these connections can be fully explained without supposing that correspondence figures in the *definition* of truth. Truth can be defined, I will maintain, in a way that is entirely in keeping with the spirit, and even the letter, of deflationism.

IV

In addition to the notion of semantic correspondence, we are in possession of a number of other *relational* semantic concepts. The members of this family include reference, denotation, and expression (i.e., the semantic concept that figures in the claim that the concept *red* expresses the property *being red*). I will be much concerned with this family in the present work.[20]

My discussion of relational semantic concepts will have three components. First, I will be concerned to show that it is possible to give illuminating characterizations of the entire range of relational concepts – characterizations that are largely deflationary in nature. Second, I will attempt to identify the sources of the practical and theoretical utility of relational concepts. Deflationists have written illuminatingly about the value of truth, but they have been comparatively silent about the value of correspondence, reference, and the rest. I will try to fill this gap. Third, I will be concerned to describe the ways in which relational semantic concepts interact with "material" or "substantive" concepts such as causation, information, and reliable indication. Many naturalistically minded philosophers have maintained that semantic concepts are somehow reducible to material concepts. As behooves a deflationist, I emphatically reject such claims. But this is a purely negative view. It is desirable to supplement it with a positive characterization of the relationship between the semantic portion of our conceptual scheme and the material portion.

Although there is some discussion of questions about relational semantic concepts in earlier chapters, the main venue for such questions is Chapter 5. I will maintain there that the utility of relational semantic concepts derives primarily from two sources. First, they provide us with the means of generating a new classificatory system, a new family of concepts that can be used in classifying thoughts and propositional attitudes. For example, they make it possible for us to pick out the class of thoughts that contain concepts that *refer to* London, or, more simply, the class of thoughts that are *about* London. Second, they make it possible for us to formulate generalizations about the relationships between propositional attitudes and extraconceptual reality. I will illustrate this second source of utility by describing the roles that the concepts play in a well confirmed theory of mental representation – specifically, that portion of commonsense psychology that describes and explains the ways in which the mind acquires information about the environment, and the ways in which the mind makes use of that information in planning and in making decisions.

As might be expected, this account of the utility of semantic concepts will also provide an answer to the question of how such concepts interact with material or substantive concepts. Thus, in considering the generalizations that constitute our commonsense theory of mental representation, we will be considering principles that connect semantic notions to a broad range of material notions, including the material notions that have figured most prominently in the attempts of philosophers to "naturalize" semantic notions. It will not be possible to enumerate all of the relevant generalizations in the present work, but I will attempt to formulate a representative sample. To the extent that this effort is successful, it will provide us with a systematic grasp of the ways in which the semantic component of our conceptual scheme is connected to the material component.

V

In addition to the topics we have been reviewing, I will also be concerned with a number of other matters, including the reasons for our involvement with states of affairs, the psychological mechanisms that enable our interpretations of indexicals, and the semantic paradoxes. For the most part, however, my discussions of these other issues will be short and exploratory, and will therefore make no claim to finality. I have set myself two tasks – that of improving the case for a deflationary construal of truth, and that of illuminating the relational notions that we use in characterizing the representational contents of concepts and thoughts. I pursue other goals only as means to these two ends.

# 2

## *Truth in the Realm of Thoughts**

This chapter presents and provides motivation for a deflationary approach to the task of analyzing semantic concepts – an approach that I call "simple substitutionalism." Simple substitutionalism is a first approximation to the approach that seems to me to be ultimately correct.

I begin with an account of Paul Horwich's theory of semantic concepts that is more comprehensive than the account offered in Chapter 1.[1] Section II argues that Horwich's account has a couple of priceless virtues, and Section III presents an argument to the effect that, despite having these virtues, Horwich's theory is badly and irreparably flawed. Together these sections show that it is desirable to seek a theory that is structurally similar to Horwich's theory (so as to share the virtues described in Section II), but that mobilizes a more powerful conceptual framework (so as to be immune to the objection formulated in Section III). Sections IV and V describe an alternative version of deflationism that meets these conditions. This alternative view, simple substitutionalism, is further elaborated in Section VI, and is defended against two particularly pressing objections in Sections VII–IX. Two appendices spell out the reasons for my claims about the virtues of simple substitutionalism in some detail.

In the present chapter I will be concerned only to explain that portion of our semantic thought and talk that is concerned with nonindexical concepts and nonindexical thoughts. This is a substantial restriction. Indexical concepts include *I, here, now, over there, yesterday, that man,* and *the woman you just mentioned.* They also include all tensed forms of verbs. As these examples suggest, indexical concepts are among the most frequently

---

*Several parts of this chapter are excerpted from the author's "Truth in the Realm of Thoughts," *Philosophical Studies* 96 (1999), 87–121.

used and the most valuable of our concepts. By the same token, indexical thoughts (thoughts that contain indexical concepts) play a large and probably essential role in our cognitive lives.

I believe that the problems posed by ascriptions of semantic concepts to indexicals can be treated without departing substantially from the spirit of the theory of ascriptions to nonindexicals that is presented here. But the issues involved are sufficiently complex to require separate treatment. I will return to them in Chapter 4.

I

As the reader may recall from Chapter 1, Horwich offers an explanation of the concept of propositional truth that is based on schema (T):

(T) The thought that $p$ is true if and only if $p$.

Thus, Horwich claims that the concept in question is implicitly defined by the class of propositions that count as substitution instances of (T). Transposing this claim, we can extend the theory by saying, for example, that when we ascribe reference to a nominal concept (i.e., to a concept whose logical properties are similar to those of a proper name), what we have in mind can be explained in terms of the following schema:

(R) For any $x$, the concept of $a$ refers to $x$ if and only if $x$ is identical with $a$.

Specifically, we can claim that the notion of reference is defined by the set of all propositions that are of form (R). We can also claim that the concept of denotation that we use in relation to monadic general concepts (i.e., in relation to concepts whose logical properties are similar to those of a monadic general term, such as "wise" or "automobile") is defined by the set of all propositions of form (D):

(D) For any $x$, the concept of a thing that is $F$ denotes $x$ if and only if $x$ is a thing that is $F$.

And, furthermore, we can make similar claims about the reference or denotation of concepts that belong to other logical categories, such as the category of dyadic general concepts.

This account of our semantic concepts is the simplest and most straightforward member of the class of deflationary theories. Indeed, it is very likely the simplest theory of truth, reference, and so on, that is possible to devise. Accordingly, it is natural to follow Horwich in referring to it as *minimalism*.

Minimalism is extremely elegant, but is there any reason for thinking that it is correct? I will now argue that the answer to this question is "yes." Specifically, I will describe grounds for thinking that it provides the best explanation for a striking fact about our beliefs of forms (T), (R), and (D) – the fact that they appear not to rest on empirical evidence.

Consider the following propositions:

(1) The thought that the universe is expanding is true if and only if the universe is expanding.
(2) For any $x$, the concept of William Jefferson Clinton refers to $x$ if and only if $x$ is identical with William Jefferson Clinton.
(3) For any $x$, the concept of a thing that is red denotes $x$ if and only if $x$ is a thing that is red.

Everyone who is possessed of the relevant concepts comes to believe these propositions as soon as he or she considers the question of whether they are true. Does the process of coming to believe them depend on empirical evidence? No. If it did, then we would come to believe them either as a result of observation or by inferring them from some well confirmed empirical theory. But it is impossible to use direct observation to establish claims about truth or reference or denotation, because none of these concepts can be said to stand for an observable property. Nor can our acceptance of (1)–(3) be due to an empirical theory.

This last contention is established – pretty conclusively, I think – by three facts. First, we feel much more certain of (1)–(3) than we do of any empirical theory. We are fully committed to (1)–(3), but insofar as we are rational, we are fallibilists about our theoretical beliefs. Second, while (1)–(3) are logically necessary, this tends not to be true of empirical theories. To be sure, as Kripke has pointed out,[2] we have some empirical beliefs that appear to be logically necessary – for example, the belief that water is $H_2O$. This group of empirical beliefs is highly circumscribed, however. The paradigm cases are limited to propositions about identity, propositions about compositional relationships, propositions about the origins of individual substances, and propositions ascribing sortals to individual substances. In general, it remains true that propositions that belong to empirical theories are logically contingent. Third, there is reason to doubt that we are in possession of an empirical theory that is capable of underwriting propositions like (1)–(3). To be sure, we are in possession of a certain number of empirically grounded generalizations about semantic properties. But these generalizations are too vague, and too limited in power, to provide a basis for generating highly specific propositions like (1)–(3). Indeed, it is much more plausible to say that our apprehension of the truth of the generalizations in question depends on our apprehension of the truth of propositions like (1)–(3) than to say that the dependence runs in the opposite direction.

It may be worthwhile to elaborate on this third point. We can, I think, claim to know a number of empirical generalizations like (4)–(7):

(4) When the relevant cognitive mechanisms are functioning properly, and the subject is in a favorable environment, sense perception is a reliable belief-forming process (in the sense that the outputs of the process tend to be true).
(5) When the relevant cognitive mechanisms are functioning properly, Baconian enumerative induction is a conditionally reliable belief-forming process (in the sense the outputs of the process tend to be true given that the corresponding inputs are true).
(6) The laws of a mature science tend to be approximately true.
(7) True beliefs about how to attain our goals tend to facilitate success in attaining them.

I have no desire to disparage generalizations like (4)–(7) – they are interesting and powerful, and there is no doubt that they are extremely useful to us when we are functioning as folk epistemologists or folk psychologists. But the present question is: Do they play a role in the process by which we come to apprehend the truth of propositions of form (T)? And I think it is reasonably clear that the answer is negative. Thus, it is clear that (4)–(7) are unable to explain our acceptance of instances of (T) by themselves. Moreover, if one considers other empirical generalizations about truth, one sees that they share the features of (4)–(7) that prevent them from providing an adequate basis for deriving the instances of (T). Thus, other generalizations are limited in subject matter to particular kinds of beliefs, or to beliefs that are used in particular ways. Equally, they suffer from the same kinds of vagueness as (4)–(7), being rife with caeteris paribus clauses and qualifications like "tends to."

On the other hand, while it is implausible to say that we come to apprehend the truth of propositions of form (T) on the basis of generalizations like (4)–(7), it is extremely plausible to say that we come to apprehend the truth of generalizations like (4)–(7) on the basis of propositions of form (T). In other words, it is extremely plausible to say that we exploit propositions of form (T) to obtain knowledge of which thoughts are true, and that we then generalize from particular facts of this sort to arrive at generalizations like (4)–(7). To see this, consider how you would react if, for example, you encountered someone who was inclined to doubt (4). Surely you would follow a procedure that involved (a) identifying a number of beliefs as products of sense perception, (b) considering what it would be like for these beliefs to be true (i.e., considering appropriate instances of (T)), (c) establishing that many of the beliefs in question were in fact true, and (d) inductively generalizing to the conclusion that (under certain conditions) beliefs produced by sense perception have a tendency to be true. You would feel entirely comfortable about proceeding in this way; and if your interlocutor seemed to be in possession of the concept of truth, you would confidently expect that he or she would fully approve of your methodology.

There is a case, then, and I think a strong case, for holding that we do not believe propositions of forms (T), (R), and (D) on the basis of empirical evidence. But if this is so, then how do we come to hold such beliefs? Minimalism provides an attractive answer to this question. According to minimalism, we come to believe propositions of the forms in question simply because they are components of definitions. If, as minimalism claims, our semantic concepts are defined by propositions of the three given forms, then anyone who possesses the concepts will *ipso facto* be disposed to believe the propositions. That is to say, one will be disposed to believe them independently of whatever empirical information one happens to possess.

It is clear, then, that minimalism can explain the fact that certain of our semantic beliefs are held independently of empirical evidence. But in addition, it is plausible – prima facie, at least – that minimalism provides the best explanation of this fact. For minimalism provides an extremely simple explanation – an explanation that makes use of no theoretical concepts beyond the concept of a definition, and makes use of no theoretical assumption other than the claim that subjects are *ipso facto* disposed to believe propositions that they know to be components of a definition. It is extremely plausible that any other explanation will commit us to a substantially greater amount of theoretical baggage.

Thus far, we have observed only that there are grounds for thinking that minimalism provides the best explanation for a certain fact. Are we in a position to go on to conclude that it does provide the best explanation? No. Whether minimalism provides the best explanation depends on whether it can be defended against objections. Perhaps there is an objection which shows that it is untenable. However, if we are not at present in a position to conclude that minimalism provides the best explanation of the foregoing fact, we are in a position to draw two conclusions that, while weaker, are nonetheless of some interest. First, we may conclude that if either minimalism itself, or any closely related theory, can be successfully defended against objections, then it should be adopted. And second, we may conclude that the following principle is a criterion of adequacy for theories of truth-conditional semantic properties: All such theories must imply that instances of (T), (R), and (D) can be known a priori, and also that they can be known with certainty and with immediacy (i.e., without laborious inference).

We now have a reason for looking on minimalism with favor. There are several other reasons for thinking well of this theory. I will conclude the present section by sketching one of them. Like the line of thought we have just concluded, this second line of thought is a best explanation argument. It maintains that minimalism provides the best explanation of the fact that skepticism about our knowledge of propositions of forms (T), (R), and (D) is absurd.

Consider the following skeptical argument: "It is clear that the following proposition strikes intuition as correct:

(8) For any $x$, the concept of a rabbit denotes $x$ if and only if $x$ is a rabbit.

But in order to have the right to claim to know that (8) is true, one must have a reason to prefer it to alternative propositions about the denotation of the concept of a rabbit. Thus, for example, it is necessary to have a reason to prefer it to (9):

(9) For any $x$, the concept of a rabbit denotes $x$ if and only if $x$ is an undetached part of a rabbit.

In fact, however, no one has a reason to prefer (8) to (9). It is impossible to rule (9) out on the basis of empirical evidence, and also impossible to refute it by an a priori argument. Hence, despite very strong intuitions to the contrary, it is erroneous to claim (8) as a piece of knowledge."[3]

This line of thought strikes us as absurd, and minimalism provides us with an explanation of this perceived absurdity. An advocate of minimalism will acknowledge that one of the claims made by the skeptic is correct. Specifically, it will be granted that our acceptance of (8) is based neither on empirical evidence nor on a priori argument. But an advocate of minimalism will claim that we have no need of evidence or an argument in order to have a right to prefer (8) to (9). The advocate will justify this claim by asserting that (8) has the status of a component of a definition. Since it is neither necessary nor appropriate to attempt to support definitional beliefs by appealing to evidence or argument, this assertion undercuts the skeptic's reasoning.

Here, then, is an explanation of the absurdity of skepticism concerning instances of (T), (R), and (D). Furthermore, since minimalism is the simplest theory that assigns a special semantic status to propositions of these forms, it is clear that the present explanation must be the simplest explanation of this absurdity.

Of course, whether it counts as the best explanation remains to be seen. The question of its ultimate adequacy depends on whether minimalism can be defended against objections. All that can be claimed at the present juncture is that it is a mark in favor of a semantic theory if it can explain the type of absurdity we have been considering, and that theories that resemble minimalism in that they assign a special semantic status to propositions of forms (T), (R), and (D) are in an extremely strong position to provide such explanations.

### III

So far so good. Now, however, we must observe that there is an objection to minimalism that appears to be insurmountable.

This objection, which was originally raised by Anil Gupta in 1993,[4] maintains that minimalism is incapable of explaining our acceptance of such a priori generalizations as (10)–(12):

(10) Only thoughts are true.
(11) For any $x$, $y$, and $z$, if $x$ is a thought that is composed of the concept *if* and two other thoughts $y$ and $z$, in that order, then $z$ is true if $x$ and $y$ are both true.
(12) For any $x$, $y$ and $z$, if $x$ is a thought that is composed of the concept *and* and two other thoughts $y$ and $z$, then $x$ is true if $y$ and $z$ are both true.

As I understand it, Gupta's justification for this contention can be summarized as follows: "If a definition of truth is to explain our acceptance of an a priori proposition, then it must be possible to derive the proposition from one or more of the clauses of which the definition is comprised. But it isn't possible to derive (10)–(12) from instances of schema (T). This is due to two facts. First, the instances of schema (T) do not include any universal generalizations about truth. They explain the conditions under which truth accrues to particular propositions, but they do not describe any general patterns of accrual or nonaccrual. Second, (10)–(12) are all universal generalizations. They describe general patterns of accrual and

nonaccrual. Now there cannot be a valid derivation of a universal generalization from a set of particular propositions unless the set in question is
inconsistent. Since every set of instances of (T) is free from contradictions
(here I prescind from the possibility that the instances of (T) may include
Liar Propositions), it follows that there cannot be a derivation leading
from instances of (T) to (10)–(12). This is a logical fact. Thus, considerations of pure logic dictate that our acceptance of (10)–(12) cannot be
explained by the definition of truth that minimalism provides."[5]

I think we must accept this reasoning as sound. Moreover, I think we
must accept Gupta's further claim that a theory of truth *should* explain
our acceptance of propositions like (10)–(12). (10)–(12) can be seen to be
correct a priori by anyone who possesses the concept of truth, provided
only that he or she also possesses the appropriate logical concepts. But
surely, if a proposition can be seen a priori to be correct on the basis of
a grasp of the concept of truth (together with a grasp of certain purely
logical concepts), then a theory that purports to specify the content of the
concept of truth should contribute substantially to the task of explaining
our acceptance of that proposition.

It turns out, then, that minimalism fails to satisfy a natural and defensible requirement of adequacy for theories of truth. We need to look
for a different theory. As we search, however, we will do well to keep
in mind the moral of Gupta's argument. In its most general version, the
moral I have in mind can be put as follows: the a priori propositions
involving the concept of truth are *data points* that a theory of truth must
explain.[6]

IV

The next theory that I wish to discuss is very close to minimalism in spirit
and content, and it therefore has the virtues we have seen minimalism to
possess. But it has an additional virtue: it is capable of explaining our
grasp of a priori generalizations like (10)–(12). This theory makes use
of a quasi-technical device – the device that has come to be known as
*substitutional quantification.*

I will begin by giving a heuristic characterization of substitutional
quantification in terms of truth. This will make it seem as though this
form of quantification is completely unsuitable for the task of explaining
what truth is, for it will suggest that any definition of truth in terms of
substitutional quantification will inevitably be circular. However, I will
soon give a second account of substitutional quantification that will free

17

it completely from any dependence on truth, and that will also show that its use is fully compatible with the spirit of traditional deflationism.

My temporary, provisional characterization of substitutional quantification consists of two principles. The first introduces the *existential substitutional quantifier*, and the second introduces the *universal substitutional quantifier*.

(13) A thought of the form $(\Sigma \mathbf{p})(\ldots \mathbf{p} \ldots)$ is true if and only if there is a thought $T$ such that the thought that results from replacing occurrences of the propositional variable $\mathbf{p}$ in the matrix $(\ldots \mathbf{p} \ldots)$ by $T$ is true.

(14) A thought of the form $(\Pi \mathbf{p})(\ldots \mathbf{p} \ldots)$ is true if and only if, for every thought $T$, the thought that results from replacing occurrences of the propositional variable $\mathbf{p}$ in the matrix $(\ldots \mathbf{p} \ldots)$ by $T$ is true.

When the quantifiers in a thought are of the ordinary objectual variety, the thought owes its truth value to facts involving extramental objects in the relevant universe of discourse. On the other hand, when the quantifiers in a thought are substitutional in character, the thought owes its truth value to certain properties of other thoughts – specifically, to the truth values of its substitution instances.

Now as noted, if we were to take the account of substitutional quantification that is afforded by (13) and (14) as final, it would be inappropriate to make use of substitutional quantification in constructing a theory of truth. The explanation offered by the theory would depend on (13) and (14), and (13) and (14) make use of the notion of truth. So the theory of truth would be circular. Fortunately, it is possible to avoid such circles by adopting a different account of substitutional quantification.

Instead of characterizing the existential and universal substitutional quantifiers by stating conditions under which thoughts containing these quantifiers are true, I propose to explain them by formulating rules of inference. It is a common practice in logic to define logical operators by describing their logical behavior. Applying this practice to the present case, I will cite rules of inference for the substitutional quantifiers that arguably capture all of the inferences involving them that we are prepared to endorse. The rules that I have in mind are counterparts of the standard rules for the familiar *objectual* quantifiers.[7] Here they are:

*Universal Elimination*

$$\frac{(\Pi \mathbf{p})(\ldots \mathbf{p} \ldots)}{(\ldots T \ldots)} \qquad \frac{(\Pi \mathbf{p})(\ldots \mathbf{p} \ldots)}{(\ldots \mathbf{q} \ldots)}$$

Here $T$ is a particular, determinate thought, and $(\ldots T\ldots)$ is the particular, determinate thought that comes from replacing all free occurrences of the propositional variable $\mathbf{p}$ in the open thought $(\ldots\mathbf{p}\ldots)$ with $T$. Further, $\mathbf{q}$ is a propositional variable, and $(\ldots\mathbf{q}\ldots)$ is the open thought that comes from replacing all free occurrences of the propositional variable $\mathbf{p}$ in the open thought $(\ldots\mathbf{p}\ldots)$ with free occurrences of $\mathbf{q}$.

*Universal Introduction*

$$\frac{(\ldots\mathbf{q}\ldots)}{(\Pi\mathbf{p})(\ldots\mathbf{p}\ldots)}$$

Here $\mathbf{q}$ is a propositional variable, and $(\ldots\mathbf{q}\ldots)$ is the open thought that comes from replacing all free occurrences of the propositional variable $\mathbf{p}$ in the open thought $(\ldots\mathbf{p}\ldots)$ with free occurrences of $\mathbf{q}$. Further, for Universal Introduction to be performed properly, $\mathbf{q}$ must satisfy two additional conditions: (i) $\mathbf{q}$ must not have a free occurrence in the thought $(\Pi\mathbf{p})(\ldots\mathbf{p}\ldots)$; and (ii) $\mathbf{q}$ must not have a free occurrence in any premise on which $(\Pi\mathbf{p})(\ldots\mathbf{p}\ldots)$ depends.

*Existential Introduction*

$$\frac{(\ldots T\ldots)}{(\Sigma\mathbf{p})(\ldots\mathbf{p}\ldots)} \qquad \frac{(\ldots\mathbf{q}\ldots)}{(\Sigma\mathbf{p})(\ldots\mathbf{p}\ldots)}$$

Here $T$ is a particular, determinate thought, and $(\ldots T\ldots)$ is the particular, determinate thought that comes from replacing all free occurrences of the propositional variable $\mathbf{p}$ in the open thought $(\ldots\mathbf{p}\ldots)$ with $T$. Further, $\mathbf{q}$ is a propositional variable, and $(\ldots\mathbf{q}\ldots)$ is the open thought that comes from replacing all free occurrences of the propositional variable $\mathbf{p}$ in the open thought $(\ldots\mathbf{p}\ldots)$ with free occurrences of $\mathbf{q}$.

*Existential Elimination*

$(\Sigma\mathbf{p})(\ldots\mathbf{p}\ldots)$

$$\frac{\text{If } (\ldots\mathbf{q}\ldots), \text{ then } T}{T}$$

Here $T$ is a thought, $\mathbf{q}$ is a propositional variable, and $(\ldots\mathbf{q}\ldots)$ is the open thought that comes from replacing all free occurrences of the propositional variable **p** in the open thought (. . . **p** . . .) with free occurrences of **q**. Further, for Existential Elimination to be properly performed, **q** must satisfy three additional conditions: (i) it cannot have a free occurrence in $T$; (ii) it cannot have a free occurrence in $(\Sigma\mathbf{p})(\ldots\mathbf{p}\ldots)$; and (iii) it cannot have a free occurrence in any premise on which the thought $T$ depends.

As I say, these rules are modeled on standard rules of inference for objectual quantifiers. In spite of this similarity, however, it is clear that they are significantly different than the latter rules, for they are concerned with variables that are altogether different than the variables that are bound by objectual quantifiers. The variables in the foregoing rules all occupy positions that can be occupied by full thoughts; the variables in rules for objectual quantifiers all occupy positions that can be occupied by nominal concepts.[8]

The foregoing rules make use of several technical concepts that are in need of explanation. But first we must consider a concept that does not occur in the rules – the concept of a *bound* occurrence of a propositional variable. Where **p** is a propositional variable, an occurrence of **p** is bound in a thought $T$ just in case it occurs within $T$ in a constituent of the form

$$(\Pi\mathbf{p})(\ldots\mathbf{p}\ldots)$$

or in a constituent of the form

$$(\Sigma\mathbf{p})(\ldots\mathbf{p}\ldots).$$

This notion enables us to define the concept of a *free* occurrence of a propositional variable, for we can say that an occurrence of **p** counts as free in a thought $T$ just in case the occurrence is not bound in $T$. Further, we can say that a context counts as *open* just in case it contains a free occurrence of some propositional variable. Here are two examples of open thoughts:

If $p$, then $(\Sigma q)$(either $q$ or it's not the case that $q$).
$(\Pi p)$(if $p$, then either $q$ or $p$).

The rules contain one more technical concept – the concept of a *particular, determinate* thought. A structure counts as a particular, determinate thought if it is a thought and it is not open.[9]

When we interpret the foregoing rules in accordance with these definitions, we find, among other things, that Universal Elimination authorizes us to make both of the following inferences:

$(\Pi p)$(if Terry believes that $p$, then $p$).

---

If Terry believes that the universe is expanding, then the universe is expanding.

$(\Pi p)$(if Terry believes that $p$, then $p$).

---

If Terry believes that $q$, then $q$.

In the first inference, the propositional variable $p$ is replaced by a particular, determinate thought, and in the second it is replaced by another propositional variable. Here a question may arise. Given that the quantifier $(\Pi p)$ is being used to express universal quantification with respect to thought contents, it is clear that it is desirable to have a rule of inference that permits inferences like our first example. But do we really need to allow for inferences like the second example? Is it useful to be able to infer open thoughts from universal quantifications? Yes. The reason is that we need a system of rules of inference that can be used to establish the validity of arguments like this one:

$(\Pi p)$(if Barry believes that $p$, then Terry believes that $p$).

$(\Pi p)$(if Terry believes that $p$, then $p$).

---

$(\Pi p)$(if Barry believes that $p$, then $p$).

In combination with Universal Introduction, Universal Elimination permits us to certify the validity of this argument by constructing the following deduction:

(1) $(\Pi p)$(if Barry believes that $p$, then Terry believes that $p$).    premise

(2) $(\Pi p)$(if Terry believes that $p$, then $p$).    premise

(3) If Barry believes that $q$, then Terry believes that $q$.    (1), Universal Elimination

(4) If Terry believes that $q$, then $q$.    (2), Universal Elimination

(5) If Barry believes that $q$, then $q$.    (3), (4), standard logic

(6) $(\Pi p)$(if Barry believes that $p$, then $p$).    (5), Universal Introduction

In formulating this derivation, I have exploited the fact that Universal Elimination permits one to infer open thoughts from universal quantifications. Without this permission, I would have wound up at line (5) with a particular, determinate thought (such as the thought that if Barry believes

21

that the Universe is expanding, then the Universe is expanding) instead of an open thought. But then I would have been unable to infer line (6) from line (5) in accordance with Universal Introduction, for Universal Introduction permits one to infer a universal quantification from another thought only when that other thought is open. (Would it be possible to change Universal Introduction in such a way as to authorize the inference to line (6) from the thought that if Barry believes that the Universe is expanding, then the Universe is expanding? No. It is intuitively incorrect to infer universal quantifications from particular, determinate thoughts.)

Two final comments. First, the rules of Universal Introduction and Existential Elimination are governed by restrictions that are not found in the formulations of Universal Elimination and Existential Introduction. I will leave these restrictions unexplained because they have no bearing on the issues that will occupy us in the present work. Suffice it to say that they are counterparts of restrictions that are standardly imposed on rules of inference for nonsubstitutional quantifiers – restrictions that can be shown to be necessary to block certain kinds of fallacy. (Explanations of these standard restrictions can be found in any good logic text (such as the one cited in footnote 7).) Second, it must be acknowledged that the apparatus of substitutional quantification may at this point seem to be largely technical in inspiration, and to have little promise as a device for explicating our commonsense intuitions about truth. I do not know whether it will be possible to assuage concerns of this sort fully, but I will argue in Section VII that there are commonsense analogues of the quantifiers we have just been considering.

V

With the apparatus of substitutional quantification in hand, it is possible to formulate a finitely axiomatized theory of truth that has all of the virtues of minimalism. This new theory, which I will call the *simple substitutional theory of truth* (or *simple substitutionalism* for short) comes to this:

(S) For any object $x$, $x$ is true if and only if $(\Sigma p)((x = \text{the thought that } p) \text{ and } p)$.

Despite consisting of only a single axiom, simple substitutionalism is extremely powerful. It is possible to infer all instances of (T) from (S). Further, it is possible to use (S) as a basis for deriving (10), and also all propositions that resemble (11) and (12) in that they spell out the truth-conditional semantic properties of logical operators.

I illustrate the power of (S) in Appendix I by using it to derive an instance of (T). I also use it to derive proposition (11) in Appendix II.[10]

As characterized thus far, simple substitutionalism offers an account of one of the central components of our commonsense theory of mental representation – the notion of truth. But it can be extended so as to offer accounts of other components of this commonsense theory – specifically, so as to offer accounts of the truth-conditional semantic properties of such parts of thoughts as singular concepts, monadic predicative concepts, and dyadic predicative concepts. It can be so extended because, in addition to substitutional quantifiers which bind variables that occupy positions appropriate to whole thoughts, there are also substitutional quantifiers which bind variables that occupy positions appropriate to singular concepts, substitutional quantifiers which bind variables that occupy positions appropriate to monadic general concepts, and so on. Putting these quantifiers to use, we can explain what it is for a singular concept to refer to an individual substance and what it is for a monadic general concept to express a property by the following principles:

(SR) For every object $x$ and every object $y$, $x$ refers to $y$ if and only if $(\Sigma a)$(the concept of $a$ is a singular concept and $x =$ the concept of $a$ and $y = a$).
(SE) For every object $x$ and every object $y$, $x$ expresses $y$ if and only if $(\Sigma F)$(the concept of a thing that is $F$ is a monadic predicative concept and $x =$ the concept of a thing that is $F$ and $y =$ the property of being an F).

By making slight changes in these principles, it is easy to obtain substitutional analyses of related semantic concepts.[11]

It seems, then, at least prima facie, that it is possible to explain a number of our semantic concepts in terms of substitutional quantification. If it turns out to be possible to sustain this view, then deflationism is vindicated. Thus, as we noticed at the outset, deflationism is the view that it is possible to explain the concept of truth and our other commonsense semantic concepts in terms of notions that carry no substantive philosophical or empirical commitments. Definitions like (S), (SR), and (SE) clearly conform to this view. In effect, such definitions reduce semantic concepts to substitutional quantification, which is a logical device. A theory that explains truth and other semantic concepts in terms of a logical device is paradigmatically deflationary.[12]

VI

Like Horwichian minimalism, simple substitutionalism can explain the a priority of instances of schemas (T), (R), and (D), and it can also explain the absurdity of semantic skepticism. But it also has another virtue: It dovetails beautifully with an extremely plausible conjecture about the role that the concept of truth plays in our descriptive and explanatory practices. Although there are anticipations in earlier writers, this conjecture appears to have been first formulated explicitly by W. V. Quine.[13]

Quine urged that truth adds no new descriptive power to our conceptual scheme, but rather enables us to make greater use of the descriptive resources that are independently available, by making it possible for us to endorse propositions that are in some sense within our ken but that we are unable to entertain explicitly or to cite by name. Quine's point may be illustrated as follows: Suppose that for some reason I wish to endorse Fermat's Last Theorem, but that I am temporarily unable to recall exactly what the Theorem asserts. Here I am unable to endorse the Theorem by explicitly asserting it, but I can nonetheless easily achieve my goal by mobilizing the concept of truth. Thus, I can achieve it by embracing the thought that Fermat's Last Theorem is *true*. According to Quine (and to Stephen Leeds, who soon joined Quine in defending this position[14]), it is in situations like this that the concept of truth finds its most characteristic employment.

This conjecture about the role of truth enjoys a considerable amount of intuitive appeal. Accordingly, if a theory of truth is in accord with it, the theory is thereby confirmed.

Now simple substitutionalism is the ideal companion for Quine's conjecture. In effect, Quine describes truth as a device that enables indefinite and generalized endorsements. But it is clear that substitutional quantifiers are paradigmatic devices of this kind! Thus, for example, using a substitutional quantifier, it is possible to frame a proposition about Fermat's Last Theorem that can serve exactly the same purposes as the foregoing proposition involving the concept of truth. To endorse the Theorem, I need only embrace the proposition $(\Sigma p)((\text{Fermat's Last Theorem} = \text{the thought that } p) \text{ and } p)$. In view of facts of this sort, it is clear that a theory that explains truth in terms of substitutional quantification implies that truth is ideally suited for the purposes that Quine mentions.[15]

VII

At this point, however, a worry may come to mind. It might seem that (S) is too foreign to our ordinary conceptual scheme for it to be plausible that it underlies our commonsense intuitions about truth. Thus, it can seem that the substitutional quantifier that figures in (S) is rather remote from the logical devices that we use in everyday life. If substitutional quantification is somewhat *outré*, then how can it be legitimate to say that substitutional quantification provides the foundation for the commonsense concept of truth?

I have three comments.

First, contrary to what the worry presupposes, it seems that substitutional quantification plays a role in our ordinary thought and discourse. Consider, for example, (15a)–(15e):

(15a) It invariably happens that when Joseph L. Camp, Jr. predicts that so-and-so, it turns out that so-and-so.

(15b) It holds in every instance that if Joseph L. Camp, Jr. believes that so-and-so, it is the case that so-and-so.

(15c) Whenever Joseph L. Camp, Jr. predicts that so-and so, then, whatever the particular nature of the prediction that so-and-so, it turns out that so-and-so.

(15d) It never fails: when Joseph L. Camp, Jr. makes a prediction with the content that so-and-so, then, whatever the particular nature of the content that so-and-so, it turns out that so-and-so.

(15e) It never fails: whenever Joseph L. Camp, Jr. predicts that so-and-so, then, whatever so-and-so may be, it turns out that so-and-so.

It is pretty clear, I think, that these propositions are well formed, and that the constituent *so-and-so* functions as a propositional variable in all of them. It is also pretty clear that *it invariably happens that* functions as a generality operator in (15a), that *it holds in every instance that* functions as a generality operator in (15b), that *whatever the particular nature of the prediction that so-and-so* functions as a generality operator in (15c), that *whatever the particular nature of the content that so-and-so* functions as a generality operator in (15d), and that *whatever so-and-so may be* functions as a generality operator in (15e). But what is the nature of these operators? Well, it is quite natural to suppose that the semantic properties of (15a)–(15e) can be explained by a principle like (14), and that their logical properties can be captured by rules that are roughly equivalent to the foregoing formulations of Universal Elimination and Universal Introduction. If these perceptions are correct, then it is appropriate to view the operators in our five propositions as substitutional quantifiers.

Second, it is possible to reformulate (S) in such a way as to reduce the sense of unfamiliarity. Thus, consider (16):

(16) For any $x$, $x$ is true if and only if for some so-and-so, (i) $x$ is identical with the thought that so-and-so, and (ii) it is the case that so-and-so.

Especially when it is considered in relation to (15a)–(15e), it is pretty clear that (16) counts as logically well formed. Moreover, reflection shows that it is quite similar to (S) in point of content. It follows that it is possible to express the content of (S) within our commonsense conceptual scheme.

Third, these points about the role of substitutional quantification can be strengthened considerably. What has been said up to now provides reason to hold that substitutional quantification is not altogether *outré*. In addition to these considerations, there are other considerations which indicate that our reliance on constructions like those in (15a)–(15e) and (16) is actually quite extensive. Thus, reflection shows that we are in possession of a number of devices that appear to play roles like the propositional quantifiers in the foregoing examples. *Generally speaking* is a case in point, as are *without fail, usually, it holds in a number of cases that*, and *it holds in at least one case that*. Furthermore, there are a number of devices that appear to play the same role as the propositional variable or "prothought" *so-and-so*. The members of this class include *things are arranged in such-and-such a way, matters stand thus and so*, and *it is so*. Combining the foregoing quantifiers with these prothoughts, we get propositions like the following:

(17) Generally speaking, when Joseph L. Camp, Jr. claims that things are arranged in such-and-such a way, things really are arranged in such-and-such a way.
(18) Without fail, when Joseph L. Camp, Jr. claims that matters stand thus and so, matters do stand thus and so.

As with the previous examples, it is natural to construe (17) and (18) as cases of substitutional quantification. (The expression "prothought" is of course modeled on "pronoun." I am here following in the footsteps of Grover, Camp, and Belnap, who formed the neologism "prosentence" to have a compact way of referring to sentential counterparts of pronouns.[16])

To be sure, the devices *things are arranged in such-and-such a way* and *matters stand thus and so* differ from *so-and-so* in that they possess complex internal structures. They are analyzable into subjects (better: prosubjects) and predicates (better: propredicates), and their predicates are analyzable into even simpler constituents. Reflecting on this fact, someone might be led to suppose that there are large-scale semantic differences between (17) and (18), on the one hand, and the earlier examples involving *so-and-so*, on the other. Thus, for example, one might be led to embrace the hypothesis that in (17), the devices *things* and *are arranged thus and so* are in fact independent variables, *things* being a plural objectual variable ranging over sequences of substances and/or events, and *are arranged in such-and-*

26

*such a way* being a property variable that ranges over complex relations that qualify as "arrangements." On this hypothesis, *generally speaking* would have a dual role in (17), figuring both as a quantifier that binds the pro-subject *things* and as a quantifier that binds the propredicate *are arranged in such-and-such a way*.

This take on (17) has a certain appeal. There are, however, a couple of considerations that count decisively against it. One is that it fails to do full justice to the meaning of (17). When I entertain (17) and give my assent to it, I understand myself to be committed to a fully general thesis about Joe Camp – one that represents him as correct in *all* his claims, however complex. I do not see myself as committed only to the thesis that Joe is correct in those of his claims that happen to have a subject-predicate structure.

Second, the position that I am defending here actually *predicts* that, in some cases, anyway, prothoughts would have complex internal structures. In particular, a subject-predicate structure enables the use of tense in formulating prothoughts (consider *things will be arranged thus and so*) and also the use of adverbs to achieve emphasis or qualification (consider *things really are arranged thus and so* and *things are not arranged thus and so*). Further, by employing devices that reflect the structures of thoughts with fully determinate meanings, one increases the formal differences between prothoughts and such other proforms as proverbs and proadjectives, thereby facilitating such cognitive operations as comparing thoughts for consistency and drawing inferences.

Counterparts of these points are familiar from the literature on pro-sentences. Thus, we find Wittgenstein making a claim that appears to be closely related to my most recent contentions in the following passage:

We may say, e.g., "He explained his position to me, said that this is how things were, and that therefore he needed an advance." So far, then, one can say that the sentence ["This is how things are"] stands for any statement. It is employed as a propositional *schema*, but *only* because it has the construction of an English sentence. It would be possible to say instead "such and such is the case," "this is the situation," and so on. It would also be possible here to use a letter, a variable, as in symbolic logic. . . .To repeat: "this is how things are" has the position only because it is itself what one calls an English sentence. But though it is a proposition, still it gets employed as a propositional variable.[17]

There are closely related passages in the writings of A. N. Prior and Dorothy Grover.[18]

I wish to turn now to consider another objection to simple substitutionalism – an objection that readers familiar with the contemporary literature
on reference are likely to think of as particularly pressing. This objection
derives from the views concerning reference and related semantic concepts that Saul Kripke and Hilary Putnam put forward in the late 1960s
and early 1970s.[19] These philosophers famously argued that the ability to
use a term to refer to an individual substance or a natural kind can depend
on certain types of causal relation between facts involving the term and
facts involving the substance or kind. As this description suggests, these
arguments were originally focused on the semantic notions we use in
connection with words, not on the notions we use in connection with
concepts. But it is widely and reasonably held that it is possible to construct similar arguments concerning semantic concepts that belong to the
latter group. Unfortunately, it seems that any such arguments would tend
to call the account of reference that is provided by simple substitutionalism
into question. For that account presupposes that the notion of conceptual
reference is altogether independent of the notion of causation.

Some of the arguments that Kripke and Putnam use are based on
elaborate thought experiments, but they also appeal to simple examples
like the following:

Someone, let's say a baby, is born; his parents call him by a certain name. They
talk about him to their friends. Other people meet him. Through various sorts of
talk the name is spread from link to link as if by a chain. A speaker who is on the
far end of this chain, who has heard about, say, Richard Feynman, in the market
place or elsewhere, may be referring to Richard Feynman even though he can't
remember from whom he first heard of Feynman or from whom he ever heard
of Feynman. He knows that Feynman is a famous physicist. A certain passage of
communication reaching ultimately to the man himself does reach the speaker.
He then is referring to Feynman even though he can't identify him uniquely. He
doesn't know what a Feynman diagram is, he doesn't know what the Feynman
theory of pair production and annihilation is. Not only that: he'd have trouble
distinguishing between Gell-Mann and Feynman. So he doesn't have to know
these things, but, instead, a chain of communication going back to Feynman
himself has been established, by virtue of his membership in a community which
passed the name on from link to link.[20]

Kripke is here reminding us of the following fact: In order for an individual to be able to use the name "Richard Feynman" to refer to the
distinguished physicist, it is sufficient that he or she be connected to

Feynman by a causal chain of reference-borrowings – a chain whose first link is the event consisting of Feynman's parents bestowing the name upon their child. Kripke allows for the possibility that an individual might be able to use a name to refer to something even though he or she was causally isolated from the thing in question, but he quite clearly favors the view that speakers are linked to referents by causal-historical chains in the normal case.

Taken collectively, the lines of thought developed by Kripke and Putnam strongly suggest that we should embrace two views about the reference of concepts. First, they suggest that whether an agent is able to refer to an individual substance in thought (i.e., to think about the substance) can depend upon whether the agent possesses a concept $C$ such that there is a causal chain linking the agent's acquisition of $C$ to the substance in question. And second, they suggest that whether an agent is able to refer to a natural kind in thought can depend upon whether the agent possesses a concept $C$ such that the agent's use of $C$ carries information about the kind in question – that is, such that the agent's use of $C$ is shaped in part by causal signals emanating from members of the kind. Since both of these views are widely accepted, I will not discuss them further here. I will simply assume that they are correct.

Moved by the views, many philosophers came to hold that there is an internal connection between the notion of reference and the notion of causation. Some even went so far as to embrace the proposition that the notion of reference can be exhaustively analyzed in terms of causation and certain other naturalistic concepts. Jerry Fodor is the paradigmatic champion of this proposition, but it has had many other defenders.[21]

Now if it is true that the notion of conceptual reference is constitutively linked to the notion of causation, then simple substitutionalism is on the wrong track. This is because simple substitutionalism represents reference and related notions as exhaustively characterizable in terms of logical notions. Thus, the account of reference that simple substitutionalism provides runs as follows:

(SR) For any object $x$ and any object $y$, $x$ refers to $y$ if and only if $(\Sigma a)$(the concept of $a$ is a singular concept and $x =$ the concept of $a$ and $y = a$).

There is of course no reference to causation in the definiens of (SR). Hence, if (SR) is accepted, we must *deny* that conceptual reference is constitutively linked to causation.

Here, then, is an objection to simple substitutionalism which seems prima facie to be quite serious. Moreover, reflection shows that this is just one member of what can only be regarded as a large family of objections. Even among those philosophers who doubt that reference is constitutively linked to causation, there is wide acceptance of the view that reference admits of a purely naturalistic characterization of *some* kind – that is, a characterization in terms of concepts drawn from mathematics and/or the natural sciences. Since (SR) makes no use of mathematical or scientific concepts, anyone who holds such a view will think there is good reason to reject simple substitutionalism.

IX

It will be helpful, I think, to begin our assessment of the foregoing objection by restating it as a formal argument:

> *First premise*: In a certain class of cases, an agent's ability to refer in thought to an individual substance or a natural kind depends constitutively upon there being causal relations that link the agent's acquisition or use of a concept to the substance or to members of the kind.
>
> *Lemma*: This connection between the ability to refer to an entity in thought and causation must be accommodated in any analysis of the concept of reference. That is to say, a successful analysis of reference must imply that, in a certain class of cases, reference constitutively involves causal relations.
>
> *Second premise*: Simple substitutionalism fails to acknowledge that conceptual reference can depend constitutively on causation.
>
> *Conclusion*: Simple substitutionalism is wrong.

When the objection is seen in this form, it becomes clear that its premises are unimpeachable.

It is nonetheless true that there is reason to reject the argument. This is because there is reason to doubt that the lemma follows from the first premise. Thus, reflection shows that the first premise and the lemma are concerned with different things. The first premise is concerned with the ability to refer to an entity in thought – that is, with a psychological capacity. The lemma, on the other hand, is not concerned with a psychological capacity but with a semantic relation that links concepts to extraconceptual entities. On the face of it, what holds of the psychological capacity could easily fail to hold of the semantic relation. In particular, it could easily be the case that it is necessary to invoke causation in explaining the psychological capacity without its being the case that it is necessary to invoke causation in explaining the semantic relation. It follows that the argument should be accorded little weight as an objection to simple substitutionalism. Perhaps it is possible to argue for the lemma on independent grounds; but taken by itself, the present argument has little if any dialectical force.

This assessment of the argument leaves us with several questions about the underlying issues. The argument is concerned with the relationships among three of our concepts: the notion of an ability to refer to an entity in thought, the notion of semantic reference, and the notion of causation. It makes certain claims about the nature of those relationships. As we have just seen, one of these claims may be wrong – anyway, the argument fails to give us a reason to accept it. But if the argument misrepresents the nature of one or more of the relationships, what is the correct way to look at them? How exactly is the notion of being able to refer to an entity in thought related to the notion of causation? And how exactly are these two notions related to the notion of semantic reference? Until we have answers to these questions, we will continue to be subject to a temptation to embrace faulty arguments like the one we have just been considering.

By way of proposing answers to these questions, I wish to recommend a theory of what is involved in being able to refer to an entity in thought that has three parts. The first part is the following definition:

(RT) For any $x$ and any $y$, $x$ is able to refer to $y$ in thought if and only if there exists a concept $C$ such that (a) $x$ possesses $C$ and (b) $C$ refers to $y$.

The second part of the theory is the claim that, in the case of many concepts, a full explanation of what is involved in possessing the concepts would necessarily involve mention of causal relations between agents who possess them and the entities to which the concepts refer. The final part is the claim that the notion of reference that figures in (b) has nothing to do with causation, and that it can in fact be analyzed correctly in the way that extended substitutionalism suggests.

Taken in combination, the first two parts of this little theory provide an attractive explanation of why it seems to us that an ability to refer to an entity in thought can depend on causal relations to extraconceptual reality. They do this by factoring each such ability into two components, a purely psychological component having to do with concept possession, and a purely semantic component, and by maintaining that it is necessary to appeal to causal relations in analyzing certain aspects of the psychological component. Now, this explanation accounts for our intuitions about the germaneness of causation to being able to refer to an entity in thought *without* postulating a connection between causation and semantic

31

reference. Hence, it provides a context in which it is appropriate to accept the third component of the theory, which denies that such a connection exists.

In short, the theory provides an alternative explanation of the data to which Kripke and Putnam call attention while honoring the claims of simple substitutionalism. It follows that we are not compelled to embrace a causal analysis of reference like the one proposed by Fodor. The data to which Kripke and Putnam call attention leave us free to accept simple substitutionalism.

The present explanation of Kripkean and Putnamian data depends crucially on the assumption that the question of whether an agent possesses a concept can depend on causal relations between the agent and the environment. But this assumption is independently plausible. Consider someone who has never directly encountered William Jefferson Clinton, and who has never received any information about Clinton in any other way, not even via a long chain of talk exchanges involving other speakers. Would it be possible for such a person to believe that Clinton was once President of the United States, or even to believe that Clinton exists? It seems that most people feel that the answers to such questions are negative. But if it is impossible for an agent who has never received any information about Clinton to form beliefs involving the concept of Clinton, then, surely, it is impossible for such a person to possess this concept. For someone who possesses a concept is automatically in a position to form beliefs involving that concept. (This topic receives further attention in Chapter 5.)

## X

We have wound up with a theory of truth that has some significant virtues. Thus, simple substitutionalism is capable of explaining our intuitions about the a priori of instances of (T), (R), and (D), and it is capable of explaining the intuition that semantic skepticism is absurd. It also honors Quine's insights about the purposes that the concept of truth is designed to serve. Furthermore, it makes use of no notions that are philosophically or empirically problematic. Still further, its chief analytic tool, the notion of substitutional quantification, is arguably similar to devices that play a role in our commonsense conceptual scheme. Thus, it is arguable that the central principles of the theory correspond, though perhaps only very roughly, to structures that are actually present in the human mind.[22] Finally, it can be shown to withstand an objection that, given the very considerable prima facie appeal of naturalistic theories of semantic properties, might reasonably be thought to be the most serious of the objections that confront it.

In view of these considerations, it seems appropriate to adopt an attitude of guarded optimism concerning the prospects of the theory.

## APPENDIX I

In this appendix, I will illustrate the generative power of (S), the core of the simple substitutional theory of truth, by using it to derive the following proposition:

(*) The thought that snow is white is true if and only if snow is white.

(*) can reasonably be taken to be a representative member of the class of instances of schema (T).

I will establish (*) by constructing two derivations, one leading from the premise *the thought that snow is white* is true to the conclusion *snow is white*, and the other moving in the opposite direction.

I will need the following two assumptions:

(S) For any $x$, $x$ is true if and only if $(\Sigma p)((x =$ the thought that $p)$ and $p)$.
(I) $(\Pi p)(\Pi q)($if the thought that $p =$ the thought that $q$, then $p$ if and only if $q)$.

Assumption (I) can be seen to be true by reflection.

### First Derivation

| | | |
|---|---|---|
| (1) | The thought that snow is white is true. | premise |
| (2) | The thought that snow is white is true if and only if $(\Sigma p)(($the thought that snow is white $=$ the thought that $p)$ and $p)$. | (S), standard logic |
| (3) | $(\Sigma p)(($the thought that snow is white $=$ the thought that $p)$ and $p)$. | (1), (2), standard logic |
| (4) | (the thought that snow is white $=$ the thought that $q)$ and $q$. | assumption for conditional proof |
| (5) | If the thought that snow is white $=$ the thought that $q$, then snow is white if and only if $q$. | (I), Universal Elimination |

33

(6) Snow is white if and only if $q$.      (4), (5), standard logic
(7) Snow is white.      (4), (6), standard logic
(8) If (the thought that snow is white      (4)–(7), conditional proof
= the thought that $q$) and $q$, then
snow is white.
(9) Snow is white.      (3), (8), Existential
     Elimination

Since this derivation satisfies all of the constraints on Existential Elimination mentioned in Section IV, we can conclude that it is correct.

Second Derivation

(1) Snow is white. [*Frozen* = $H_2O$ is white] premise
(2) The thought that snow is white =      logic of identity
the thought that snow is white. [*if it exists*.]
(3) (the thought that snow is white      (1), (2), standard logic
= the thought that snow is white)
and snow [*How*] is white.
(4) $(\Sigma p)$((the thought that snow is      (3), Existential
white = the thought that $p$) and      Introduction
$p$)
(5) The thought that snow is white      (S), standard logic
is true if and only if $(\Sigma p)$((the
thought that snow is white = the
thought that $p$) and $p$).
(6) The thought that snow is white is      (4), (5), standard logic
true.

*[marginalia: "? in depth on 1,2, EI (4) and 5."]*

APPENDIX II

In this appendix I will show how to use (S) to prove the following generalization:

For any $x$, $y$, and $z$, if $x$ is a thought that is composed of the concept *if* and the thoughts $y$ and $z$, in that order, then $z$ is true if $x$ and $y$ are both true.

I take the following to be a reasonable translation of this generalization:

(@) $(\forall x)(\forall y)$(if ($x$ is a thought and $y$ is a thought and $x$ is true and $cond(x, y)$ is true), then $y$ is true).

Here "*cond*" stands for an operator that maps each pair of thoughts onto the thought consisting of the concept *if* and the first and second components of the pair (in that order). The only premises I will need are (S) and (I)–(III):

(S) $(\forall x)(x$ is true if and only if $(\Sigma p)((x = $ the thought that $p)$ and $p))$.
(I) $(\forall x)($if $x$ is a thought, then $(\Sigma p)(x = $ the thought that $p))$.
(II) $(\forall x)(\forall y)(\Pi p)(\Pi q)($if $(x = $ the thought that $p$ and $y = $ the thought that $q)$, then cond$(x, y) = $ the thought that if $p$ then $q)$.
(III) $(\Pi p)(\Pi q)($if the thought that $p = $ the thought that $q$, then $p$ if and only if $q)$.

Here (I)–(III) are axioms of the theory of thoughts. Each can be seen to be true by reflection.

A comment about notation: I have found that, in the context of the following argument, expressions of the form "the thought that if $p$ then $q$" can be confusing. I will accordingly use expressions of the form "the thought that $p \rightarrow q$" in their place.

We can now proceed to the proof of (@). It runs as follows:

| | |
|---|---|
| (1) $a$ is a thought. | premise |
| (2) $b$ is a thought. | premise |
| (3) $a$ is true. | premise |
| (4) cond$(a, b)$ is true. | premise |
| (5) If $a$ is a thought, then $(\Sigma p)$ $(a = $ the thought that $p)$. | (I), standard logic |
| (6) $(\Sigma p)(a = $ the thought that $p)$. | (1), (5), standard logic |
| (7) If $b$ is a thought, then $(\Sigma p)$ $(b = $ the thought that $p)$. | (I), standard logic |
| (8) $(\Sigma p)(b = $ the thought that $p)$. | (2), (7), standard logic |
| (9) $a = $ the thought that $r$. | assumption for conditional proof |
| (10) $b = $ the thought that $s$. | assumption for conditional proof |
| (11) If $(a = $ the thought that $r$ and $b = $ the thought that $s)$, then cond$(a, b) = $ the thought that $r \rightarrow s$. | (II), standard logic, Universal Elimination |
| (12) cond$(a, b) = $ the thought that $r \rightarrow s$. | (9), (10), (11), standard logic |
| (13) The thought that $r \rightarrow s$ is true. | (4), (12), substitutivity of identity |

| | |
|---|---|
| (14) The thought that $r$ is true. | (3), (9), substitutivity of identity |
| (15) The thought that $r \rightarrow s$ is true if and only if $(\Sigma p)((\text{the thought that } r \rightarrow s = \text{the thought that } p) \text{ and } p)$. | (S), standard logic |
| (16) $(\Sigma p)((\text{the thought that } r \rightarrow s = \text{the thought that } p) \text{ and } p)$. | (13), (15), standard logic |
| (17) The thought that $r$ is true if and only if $(\Sigma p)((\text{the thought that } r = \text{the thought that } p) \text{ and } p)$. | (S), standard logic |
| (18) $(\Sigma p)((\text{the thought that } r = \text{the thought that } p) \text{ and } p)$. | (14), (17), standard logic |
| (19) (the thought that $r \rightarrow s = \text{the thought that } p)$ and $p$. | assumption for cond. proof |
| (20) (the thought that $r = \text{the thought that } q)$ and $q$. | assumption for cond. proof |
| (21) If the thought that $r \rightarrow s = \text{the thought that } p$, then $r \rightarrow s$ if and only if $p$. | (III), Universal Elimination |
| (22) $r \rightarrow s$ if and only if $p$. | (19), (21), standard logic |
| (23) If the thought that $r = \text{the thought that } q$, then $r$ if and only if $q$. | (III), Universal Elimination |
| (24) $r$ if and only if $q$. | (20), (23), standard logic |
| (25) $r \rightarrow s$. | (19), (22), standard logic |
| (26) $r$. | (20), (24), standard logic |
| (27) $s$. | (25), (26), standard logic |
| (28) The thought that $s = \text{the thought that } s$. | reflexivity of identity |
| (29) (the thought that $s = \text{the thought that } s)$ and $s$. | (27), (28), standard logic |
| (30) $(\Sigma p)((\text{the thought that } s = \text{the thought that } p) \text{ and } p)$. | (29), Existential Introduction |
| (31) The thought that $s$ is true if and only if $(\Sigma p)((\text{the thought that } s = \text{the thought that } p) \text{ and } p)$. | (S), standard logic |
| (32) The thought that $s$ is true. | (30), (31), standard logic |
| (33) $b$ is true. | (10), (32), substitutivity of identity |

(34) If ((the thought that $r =$ the thought that $q$) and $q$), then $b$ is true.

(20)–(33), conditional proof

(35) $b$ is true.

(18), (34), Existential Elimination

(36) If ((the thought that $r \rightarrow s =$ the thought that $p$) and $p$), then $b$ is true.

(19)–(35), conditional proof

(37) $b$ is true.

(16), (36), Existential Elimination

(38) If $b =$ the thought that $s$, then $b$ is true.

(10)–(37), conditional proof

(39) $b$ is true.

(8), (38), Existential Elimination

(40) If $a =$ the thought that $r$, then $b$ is true.

(9)–(39), conditional proof

(41) $b$ is true.

(6), (40), Existential Elimination

(42) If ($a$ is a thought and $b$ is a thought and $a$ is true and $cond(a, b)$ is true), then $b$ is true.

$[(1) + (2) + (3) + (4)]$–(41), conditional proof

(43) (@)

(42), standard logic

Since all of the restrictions on Existential Elimination are observed in each of the four applications of that rule, the proof is correct.

# 3

## *The Marriage of Heaven and Hell:*
## Reconciling Deflationary
## Semantics with Correspondence
## Intuitions*

Simple substitutionalism maintains that the content of the concept of truth is fully captured by the following explicit definition:

(S) For any $x$, $x$ is true if and only if $(\Sigma p)((x = $ the thought that $p)$ and $p)$,

where $\Sigma$ stands for existential substitutional quantification. It also asserts that it is possible to give similar explanations of other semantic concepts. Thus, among other things, simple substitutionalism asserts that the concepts of reference and expression can be defined as follows:

(SR) For any object $x$ and any object $y$, $x$ refers to $y$ if and only if $(\Sigma a)$(the concept of $a$ is a singular concept and $x = $ the concept of $a$ and $y = a$).
(SE) For any object $x$ and any object $y$, $x$ expresses $y$ if and only if $(\Sigma F)$(the concept of a thing that is $F$ is a monadic general concept and $x = $ the concept of a thing that is $F$ and $y = $ the property of being an $F$).

As we saw in the last chapter, simple substitutionalism has some extremely important virtues.

### SECTION II: AN OBJECTION TO CLASSICAL DEFLATIONISM

Unfortunately, despite its virtues, simple substitutionalism appears to be at odds with certain of our intuitions about truth. Thus, it appears that

---

*Several sections of this chapter are excerpted from an earlier paper of mine ("The Marriage of Heaven and Hell: Reconciling Deflationary Semantics with Correspondence Intutions,"*Philosophical Studies* 104 (2001), 289–321), and several other sections are adapted from that paper.

we have intuitions to the effect that, in a wide range of cases, thoughts mirror or correspond to extraconceptual circumstances, and that within this range of cases, when a thought counts as true, it does so in virtue of the fact that the corresponding circumstance actually obtains. In other words, it appears that we have intuitions about truth that can appropriately be called *correspondence intuitions*. Now this description of the intuitions in question is pretty vague. Even without getting clearer about their content, however, it is plausible that they point to the existence and importance of a semantic concept that is not recognized by theories that count as versions of deflationism. Thus, the intuitions indicate that we are in possession of a concept that stands for a relation linking thoughts to the world – a concept of mental mirroring or semantic correspondence. As formulated above, simple substitutionalism makes no mention of such a concept. Nor does any other deflationary theory. Accordingly, there is reason to fear that our correspondence intuitions may call simple substitutionalism and its deflationary colleagues into question.

There is a way of sharpening these points that has enjoyed considerable support, both within philosophy and without. Thus, it has often been claimed that we are in possession of intuitions which show that we are committed to the correspondence theory of truth, or in other words, to (CT):

(CT) For any thought $x$, $x$ is true if and only if there is a state of affairs $y$ such that (a) $x$ semantically corresponds to $y$, and (b) $y$ actually obtains.

More: It has often been claimed that these intuitions show that (CT) is definitional with respect to truth – that the concept of truth bears roughly the same relation to (CT) as the concept of a bachelor bears to the principle that bachelors are unmarried adult males.

Now it is clear that (CT) is at variance with simple substitutionalism and with Horwich's theory of truth. Neither of these theories represents truth as depending on a relation between thoughts and the world, nor do they make any mention of states of affairs. But more: It is clear that (CT) is at variance with *every* theory that counts as a version of classical deflationism. Talk of mental mirroring, states of affairs, and actuality drives deflationists wild! Indeed, although there are several other reasons for embracing classical deflationism, it appears that a number of philosophers have been drawn to it precisely because they have given up on the project of finding adequate explications of mental mirroring, states of affairs, and actuality.

There are grounds, then, for thinking that we have intuitions that pose a threat to deflationism in general and to simple substitutionalism in particular. But it remains to be seen whether these grounds can stand up to critical assessment. Perhaps it must be conceded that we have intuitions that can appropriately be called "correspondence intuitions." But what exactly do these intuitions show? Do they show that we are committed to (CT)? Or only that we are committed to a weaker principle? Or to a principle that has a higher degree of vagueness? Furthermore, even if it were conceded that we have intuitions that commit us to (CT), it would remain open whether those intuitions should be accorded much weight. Perhaps the commitment they reveal is unimportant and easily discarded. Perhaps they are associated with patterns of thought that are only superficially or tangentially related to the main concerns of commonsense semantics. All of these issues must be investigated before we can understand the real significance of our correspondence intuitions, or assess their relationship to simple substitutionalism.

As will become clear in the sequel, I hold that our correspondence intuitions are deeply and multiply grounded in our commonsense conceptual scheme, and that it is therefore appropriate to assign considerable evidentiary weight to them when one is concerned to describe the structure and content of our commonsense semantic concepts. Furthermore, I think that the intuitions do in fact show that simple substitutionalism and all other unqualifiedly deflationary theories are inadequate. It is important to distinguish, however, between two forms of inadequacy. A theory can be inadequate because it is wrong, and it can also be inadequate because it is incomplete. As I see it, simple substitutionalism is characterized only by the second form of inadequacy. Thus, as I see it, correspondence intuitions have no tendency to show that simple substitutionalism's definitions of truth and other semantic concepts are mistaken. Rather, they show that simple substitutionalism fails to tell the *whole* truth about commonsense semantics. More concretely, they show that simple substitutionalism suffers from two forms of incompleteness, one that is ideological in character, and another that is more properly described as doctrinal. It is ideologically incomplete because it fails to acknowledge the existence of the notion of semantic correspondence, and it is doctrinally incomplete because it fails to recognize that there is an important tie (a tie that is a priori though not definitional) between this notion and the concept of truth.

In this chapter, I will be concerned with the task of developing and defending these views. The next six sections will focus on questions about the provenience, content, and evidentiary significance of our

correspondence intuitions. I will attempt to show that the var
cepts that figure in (CT) – the concept of a state of affairs, the c
semantic correspondence, and the concept of actuality – occup'
of importance within our conceptual scheme, and also that the
principles that virtually force us to see them as closely related to one another and as closely related also to the concept of truth. Then, building on
these conclusions, I will attempt to describe a theoretical perspective that
in effect blends them with the main claims of simple substitutionalism.

### SECTION III: STATES OF AFFAIRS

Turning now to the first of these responsibilities, I must begin by begging
the reader's indulgence. The present section will be rather long, comparatively speaking, and it will be concerned with issues that are not immediately relevant to questions about truth. It appears, however, that this
is one of those occasions on which it is desirable to choose a route that
is somewhat circuitous. If it is true, as it seems prima facie to be, that
the notion of a state of affairs figures prominently in our correspondence
intuitions, then it is impossible to assess the force of the intuitions without
investigating questions about the salience and stability of our commitment
to states of affairs. But any investigation of such questions – even a su-
perficial one – must concern itself with a number of issues that are not
directly pertinent to semantic questions.

It appears that the modal dimension of our conceptual scheme is one
of the primary sources of our intuitions about states of affairs. As many
authors have noted, it is extremely plausible that this dimension carries a
commitment to *possibilities* – that is, to such things as possible courses of
events (including possible courses of action), possible outcomes, and possible situations. Thus, we are strongly inclined to accept such propositions
as these: *there are several possible courses of action that are open to me, there are
several possible outcomes of my decision that would cause me to feel regret*, and
*there are a number of situations in which I might find myself today for which I am
totally unprepared.* Now these propositions invite the following question:
is there a single metaphysical category, or a single family of categories,
that encompasses the whole range of possibilities? That is to say, is there a
single category, or a single family of categories, to which such entities as
possible courses of events, possible outcomes, and possible situations can
all be said to belong? It is pretty clear, I think, that the answer is "yes."
More concretely, it is pretty clear that possibilities generally belong to the
various categories that are associated with the notion of a possible state of

affairs – that is to say, the category consisting of states of affairs, and the category consisting of sets of states of affairs, and the category consisting of types of states of affairs, and the category consisting of sets of types of states of affairs. To appreciate the plausibility of this answer, consider the task of describing the outcome of a certain possible course of events. In order to capture the distinctive nature of a particular outcome, one must do more than list the objects that are involved in the outcome. Nor would it be enough to list these objects together with the properties that they instantiate. In addition, one must list the *relationships of instantiation* that link the objects in question to the properties in question. In other words, to do justice to the particularities of the outcome, one must view it as a complex entity whose constituents are *property-exemplifications*. But this means that one must view it as a state of affairs (or perhaps, as a set of states of affairs).

It appears, then, that we are committed to the existence of possibilities, and that this commitment is plausibly construed as a commitment to states of affairs (and to certain related entities, such as sets of states of affairs). It follows that our commitment to states of affairs is such as to give them a position of prominence in our conceptual scheme. For possibilities figure prominently in practical and theoretical endeavors that are of great importance to us: We are involved with possibilities when we are engaged in planning, and when we are engaged in making statistical predictions, and when we are engaged in counterfactual and other forms of subjunctive reasoning.

Does our commitment to an ontology of states of affairs have any other sources? There is good reason to think that the answer should be "yes." Thus, it appears to be built into our commonsense picture of causes and effects that it is property-exemplifications, not substances or properties, that are the terms of the relation of singular causation. Consider, for example, our views about the causal history of the death of John F. Kennedy. We are willing to say that Kennedy's death was caused by a bullet, but in making this claim, we view it as an elliptical version of the claim that the death was caused by the bullet's striking Kennedy. It is always thus: when we consider a fact involving singular causation, we find it natural and even inevitable to see it as a complex structure involving a relation and two states of affairs. Since we see relationships of singular causation as existing everywhere, and as being of great importance both for the universe in general and for ourselves in particular, it is not surprising that references to property-exemplifications pervade ordinary thought and discourse.

In making these claims about singular causation I am giving expression to perceptions that are widely shared. It must be acknowledged, however, that there is an alternative picture of singular causation that also enjoys wide acceptance. This is the view that the terms of the relation of singular causation are *events* rather than states of affairs, where events are understood to be concrete particulars. This view acknowledges that we use a variety of locutions in talking about causal relations, including locutions which strongly suggest that causes and effects are states of affairs; but it maintains that causal relationships are most accurately depicted by claims like "Don's fall caused Don's death" and "Sarah's menacing gesture contributed to Fred's distress," and it construes the singular terms that figure in such claims (e.g., "Don's death") as descriptions or names of concrete particulars. If asked how concrete events differ from states of affairs, an advocate of this picture would respond that the principles governing the individuation of the former entities are less restrictive than the principles governing the individuation of the latter entities. Thus, it would be said, for example, that if Sarah menaces Fred by shaking her fist at him, then the concrete event we pick out by the description "Sarah's menacing gesture" is identical with the concrete event we pick out by the description "Sarah's shaking a fist." This separates the event in question from states of affairs, for it would be a mistake to suppose that the state of affairs we pick out by the description "the state of affairs consisting of Sarah's gesturing in a menacing way" is identical with the state of affairs we pick out by the description "the state of affairs consisting of Sarah's shaking a fist." (In general, the state of affairs determined by one description is distinct from the state of affairs determined by a second description if the property invoked by the first description is distinct from the property invoked by the second description. The property invoked by the description "the state of affairs consisting of Sarah's making a menacing gesture" is the property of making a menacing gesture, while the property invoked by "the state of affairs consisting of Sarah's shaking a fist" is the property of shaking a fist. The former property is of course distinct from the latter property.)

This alternative picture of causation, which has been developed with subtlety and insight by Davidson and his followers,[1] is supported by a variety of linguistic data, and also receives a certain amount of direct support from our intuitions about singular causation. It would take us too far afield to attempt to assess these supporting considerations here.[2] Accordingly, instead of discussing them, I will simply point to an opposing line of thought that seems – to me, at least – to have considerably greater force.

Let us return to our original paradigm: the cause picked out by the description "the bullet's striking Kennedy." When we reflect on this cause, we find, I believe, that it is extremely natural to think of it as a state of affairs. Thus, clearly, for any possible spatiotemporal context $C$, the cause fails to exist in $C$ unless the relevant bullet exists in $C$ and Kennedy exists in $C$. This fact makes a strong case for the claim that the bullet and Kennedy are both implicated in the identity conditions of the cause, and this claim in turn makes a strong case for the claim that the bullet and Kennedy count as constituents of the cause. But we cannot say that they are the only constituents; for if we were to say this, we would be flouting the perception that the cause under consideration is quite different from certain other causes in which the bullet and Kennedy are involved, such as the cause picked out by the description "the bullet's speeding toward Kennedy." Evidently, the relation of striking must also be a constituent of the cause. But we still do not have a fully adequate picture of the cause in question. That is to say, the cause cannot be fully specified by listing these three constituents. We must also say that the cause has a structure which makes it true that it is a case of a bullet striking Kennedy rather than a case of Kennedy striking a bullet. Thus, to sum up, it is plausible that the cause we are considering has three constituents – two substances and a relation– and that it has a structure which reflects one rather than the other of the two ways in which the relation in question can be instantiated by the two substances. Further, when we consider claims to the effect that the consituents of the cause include additional physical objects, or additional relations, we find that they seem less well motivated than this one. Accordingly, it is plausible that the cause just *is* the state of affairs consisting of the given objects and the given relation arranged in the given way.

If we adopt this view about the nature of our paradigmatic cause, what should we say about such Davidsonian causes as Don's fall and Sarah's minatory gesture? As in the case of our paradigmatic cause, I am inclined to think that substances, properties, and relationships of instantiation are implicated in the identity conditions of these entities, and that it is therefore entirely natural to think of these entities as property-exemplifications.

To conclude: There are features of our quotidian thought and talk about causation which suggest that we are strongly disposed to think of causes and effects as states of affairs. Moreover, these features have their home on the surface of our thought and talk: descriptions like "the bullet's striking Kennedy" are ubiquitous, and they lead to the conclusion that causes and effects are states of affairs by natural lines of thought.

Our involvements with possibility and causation are deeply rooted in our practical needs and interests. Since these involvements carry a commitment to states of affairs, it is natural to conclude that our involvement with states of affairs has a practical dimension. But this is only part of the story: It is also true that there is a purely metaphysical dimension to our involvement with states of affairs. This is because we are disposed to have "metaphysical intuitions" about the world as a whole that carry a commitment to such entities. What I have in mind here are perceptions to the effect that the world as a whole is a complex, organized structure that is analyzable into progressively smaller constituents. When combined with a few supplementary principles that are uncontroversial, these perceptions lead quickly to the conclusion that the world is a system of interlocking states of affairs.

Even though metaphysical intuitions of the sort in question are somewhat remote from the fabric of everyday life, they strike us as quite compelling on those occasions when we experience them. So let us assume that they are valid. Now there are several ways of analyzing the world into constituents. Thus, it is possible to think of the world as consisting of objects, and it is also possible to think of it as "containing" the properties that have instances in it. But there is also a third way of analyzing the world: one can think of it as composed of complex entities in which both objects and properties are involved – that is, as composed of objects-as-characterized-by-properties. In short, it is possible to think of it as composed of states of affairs. Now this third way of analyzing the world is not reducible to either of the others, nor even to the pair consisting of both of the other ways. For no list of objects or of properties, and no pair of such lists, can uniquely determine a set of (contingent) states of affairs. On the other hand, a list of the states of affairs that count as constituents of the world would uniquely determine both the objects that exist in the world and the properties that characterize those objects. Accordingly, an analysis of the world into states of affairs may be said to be the only type of analysis that can *capture the distinctive nature of the world* – the only type that can succeed in distinguishing the actual world from the infinite host of other possible worlds. By the same token, analyses of the sort in question deserve (and receive) a position of privilege in our intuitive vision of the world as a complex, organized totality.[3]

Here, then, is a third source of the idea that an inventory of reality would have to include states of affairs. I believe there are other sources.[4] But the present three suffice to establish that the idea is both deeply and multiply grounded in important human concerns. By the same token, they suffice to remind us that the impression that states of affairs exist is a vivid one, and that it is stable across a variety of perspectives that it is natural for us to assume. In short, they remind us of the *salience* of states of affairs.

Perhaps it will be helpful to conclude the present section with a summary and a look ahead. The ultimate goal is to improve our understanding of our correspondence intuitions, that is, our intuitions to the effect that there are significant connections between the concept of truth and the concept of a mirroring or correspondence relation that links thought to extraconceptual reality. Now it is widely held, and it seems to me to be true, that the mirroring relation in question could only be a relation that links thoughts to states of affairs. Accordingly, if we are to identify the sources of our correspondence intuitions, and to appreciate the stability of these sources, it is important to explain how we come by the notion of a state of affairs, and also to explain why we suppose this notion to stand for a class of real entities. In the present section we have been concerned to find such explanations, and thereby, to take the first step toward our ultimate goal. It is time now to take the second step, which is to describe the form and content of the concepts that we use when we wish to make reference to specific states of affairs.

### SECTION IV: CANONICAL NAMES FOR STATES OF AFFAIRS

Our canonical names for states of affairs fall into two main categories. One category consists of concepts that are actuality-neutral, in the sense that it is possible to use them without being committed to claims to the effect that their referents actually obtain. This category includes concepts of the form *the state of affairs that obtains just in case p*, concepts of the form *the possibility that p*, concepts of the form *the state of affairs $*p*$*, where $*p*$ is a nominalization of the thought content $p$ (in the way that *Judas's betrayal of Jesus* and *Judas's betraying Jesus* are nominalizations of *Judas betrays Jesus*), concepts of the form *the situation consisting of $*p*$*, and concepts of the form $*p*$. The other category consists of concepts that carry commitments concerning the actuality of states of affairs. It includes concepts of the form *the fact that p* and concepts of the form *its being the case that p*.

It is a striking fact that all of these devices have thought contents as constituents. The contents may have been subjected to various nominalizing transformations, but the transformations in question are never such as to delete conceptual building blocks or to distort logical relationships. The original contents always shine through.

My main concern here is simply to call attention to this phenomenon, for it will be at the heart of the discussion in the following section; but I would also like to propose an explanation of it. The explanation I have in mind consists of two claims, one that is concerned with canonical names of the first type (that is, with names whose use does not carry a presupposition of actuality), and another that is concerned with canonical names of the second type (that is, with names that do carry a presupposition of actuality). The first claim is the hypothesis that canonical names of the first type are equivalent in content to definite descriptions of the form *the state of affairs x such that, necessarily, x is actual if and only if p*. The second claim is the hypothesis that canonical names of the second type are equivalent in content to definite descriptions of the form *the actually obtaining state of affairs x such that, necessarily, x is actual if and only if p*. Taken together, these claims provide a full answer to the question, "What is the nature of the logical role that thought contents play when they serve as constituents of canonical names?" They answer this question by asserting that thought contents enable canonical names to pick out particular states of affairs by specifying the conditions under which states of affairs are actual. More fully, they assert that thought contents enable reference to states of affairs by figuring in biconditionals that give necessary and sufficient conditions for the actuality of states of affairs.[5]

Canonical names are on the whole quite different in surface structure from complex descriptions of the foregoing forms, so the present account of the meanings of canonical names is in need of justification. But there are in fact two good reasons for embracing it. One is that the account explains the roles that thought contents play in canonical names in terms of constructions that are familiar from basic modal logic. Because of this feature of the account, it can be said to explain an otherwise mysterious phenomenon in terms of constructions that are well understood, and that are known on independent grounds to figure in our conceptual scheme. A theory that explains a mystery in terms of independently motivated constructions is *ipso facto* one that deserves respect. Second, the account provides a foundation for explaining the validity of a range of inferences. Examples include inferences of the following forms:

The possibility that $p$ is actual
$$\frac{}{p}$$

The state of affairs $^*p^*$ is actual
$$\frac{}{p}$$

If we assume that the premises of such inferences have the meanings that the account attributes to them, we can explain the validity of the inferences without appealing to any principles other than the basic rules of deductive logic – rules that are known to exist on independent grounds. Otherwise, we would have to settle for an explanation that involves a variety of special purpose assumptions, assumptions that would inevitably seem ad hoc.

So much for doctrine. I would like now to simplify matters by adopting the policy of focusing exclusively on canonical names that do not carry a presupposition of actuality. Thus, I will hereafter prescind from canonical names like *the fact that p*. It will, I think, be clear that one would encounter no insurmountable difficulties in attempting to extend the doctrines put forward in later sections to canonical names of the latter sort. Furthermore, I would like to introduce a notational convention. As we observed, even within the restricted class consisting of names that are actuality-neutral, canonical names for states of affairs can take a variety of forms. In the interests of simplicity, I propose hereafter to use concepts of the form *the state of affairs that p* to represent all of the members of this highly variegated family. Thus, I will generally write as if concepts of the given form were our only canonical names for states of affairs. Among other things, this will make it possible to formulate generalizations about canonical names as single, unified claims. Otherwise it would be necessary in each case to put forward a number of different generalizations, one for each of the forms that canonical names can take.

## SECTION V: SEMANTIC CORRESPONDENCE

Turning now to the topic of semantic correspondence, I would like to begin by calling attention to a formal relationship between our canonical names for thoughts and our canonical names for states of affairs. We have a practice of using concepts of the form *the thought that p* as canonical names for thoughts, and a practice of using concepts of the form *the state of affairs that p* as canonical names for states of affairs. It follows that each canonical name for a thought is connected to a canonical name for a state of affairs by a formal relation – the relation *having the same thought as a constituent*. Thus, for example, the canonical name *the thought that snow is white* bears this relation to the canonical name *the state of affairs that snow is white*, for these names both have the thought *snow is white* as a constituent.

As this example shows, facts involving the relation in question are highly salient. It could hardly escape our attention that the name *the thought that snow is white* bears the relation to the name *the state of affairs that snow is white*.

Now this formal relation between canonical names induces a relation between thoughts and states of affairs. More concretely, it induces a relation $R$ that satisfies the following condition: Where $x$ is any thought and $y$ is any state of affairs, $x$ bears $R$ to $y$ if and only if $x$ and $y$ have canonical names $N_1$ and $N_2$, respectively, such that $N_1$ bears the formal relation *having the same thought as a constituent* to $N_2$. This induced relation will of course inherit the salience of the given formal relation.

There is another way to characterize $R$, a way that is at once more elegant and less vague. The characterization I have in mind makes use of substitutional quantification. It runs as follows:

(SC) For any thought $x$ and any state of affairs $y$, $x$ bears $R$ to $y$ if and only if $(\Sigma p)(x =$ the thought that $p$ and $y =$ the state of affairs that $p$).

This characterization will figure prominently in our later reflections.[6]

It is natural, I believe, to say that the relationship that is specified by (SC) is the intuitive relation of semantic correspondence. After all, $R$ involves exactly those pairs that we think of as linked by mental mirroring or semantic correspondence. And it is quite plausible that we have no grasp on the intuitive relation of correspondence other than via the fact that it is a relation that involves the pairs in question. (If you were asked to explain semantic correspondence, you would almost certainly say something like the following: "It is the relation that links the thought that Caesar crossed the Rubicon and the state of affairs that Caesar crossed the Rubicon, the thought that Washington crossed the Delaware and the state of affairs that Washington crossed the Delaware, and so on." If these examples did not work, you would be quite at a loss as to how to replace your explanation with a better one.)

Now as I see it, informal counterparts of the substitutional quantifiers are included in our commonsense stock of logical devices. (See Section VII of Chapter 2.) And of course, if this view is right, it is entirely appropriate to claim that (SC) is available from a commonsense perspective. So I make this claim. Further, I wish to claim that something like (SC) is the source of our intuitive notion of semantic correspondence. That is to say, (SC) (or something very much like it) is definitional with respect to the intuitive notion of semantic correspondence.

(SC) has a number of implications that seem entirely correct. Thus, as we have already observed, it implies that the relation of semantic correspondence is highly salient. It also implies that our apprehension of semantic correspondence is a priori, and that propositions of the form *the thought that p semantically corresponds to the state of affairs that p* are logically necessary. Finally, it implies that our involvement with semantic correspondence is deeply rooted in our conceptual scheme. Thus, as we have seen, an awareness of the relation that is picked out by (SC) is in effect forced on us by certain of our practices involving canonical names. It is obvious that those practices have roots that are deep and permanent.

So far so good. We now have an account of the content and sources of the notion of semantic correspondence. Moreover, we are in a position to understand why the notion can strike us as natural and unavoidable. If the present account of it is correct, then the notion is defined in terms of the following five devices: conjunction, identity, the existential substitutional quantifier, the operator *the thought that*, and the operator *the state of affairs that*. The first three of these devices belong to logic, and are therefore free from empirical and metaphysical presuppositions. The operator *the thought that* is simply a device for forming canonical names for thoughts.[7] It presupposes a complex theory – the theory of propositional attitudes that is built into folk psychology. But that theory is entirely familiar, and is recommended to us by its great predictive and explanatory power. Finally, the operator *the state of affairs that* presupposes the theory of states of affairs that is built into folk metaphysics. It cannot be said that the theory is unproblematic. As we noticed in Section II, however, it appears that we are committed to that theory by deep-seated practical and metaphysical concerns.

In view of the fact that it is virtually forced on us by certain of our procedures for constructing names, it is clear that the notion of semantic correspondence is here to stay. But more: In virtue of the fact that it can be fully characterized in terms of notions drawn from logic and other notions that appear to be extremely well motivated, it is natural to suppose that the notion of correspondence deserves this stability.

We have, then, arrived at a preliminary characterization of semantic correspondence. It remains to determine exactly how this notion is related to the concept of truth. Before we can begin to explore that further question, however, we must consider the relationship between the concept of truth and the concept of actuality. This relationship is the topic of the next section.[8]

Although there is much about the nature of the concept of actuality that is highly controversial, there is one thesis about the concept that appears incontestable. This is the thesis that every thought that can be obtained from the following schema by substitution has a claim on our assent:

(A) If the state of affairs that $p$ exists, then the state of affairs that $p$ is actual if and only if $p$.

Here, of course, the notion of existence is taken to have a much broader compass than the notion of actuality: existence is taken to be a property of *all* states of affairs, including those that are merely possible, while actuality is taken to be a property that is exhibited only by those states of affairs that can be said to obtain in the actual world.[9]

It is interesting that this one fact about actuality suffices to explain why there is an a priori connection between actuality and truth. Thus, whatever else one believes about truth, one will certainly believe that we are disposed to embrace all thoughts that are instances of schema (T):

(T) The thought that $p$ is true if and only if $p$.

But when they are combined with the appropriate instances of (A), instances of (T) imply thoughts that are instances of (AT):

(AT) If the state of affairs that $p$ exists, then the thought that $p$ is true if and only if the state of affairs that $p$ is actual.

It follows that we are disposed to embrace every instance of (AT). But to say this is to say that there is a deep and systematic relationship between truth and actuality.

Now of course, the claim that there is a deep and systematic connection between truth and actuality is part of the content of the correspondence theory of truth. Thus, since instances of (A) are partly responsible for the plausibility of (AT), it appears that they are also partly responsible for the intuitions that seem to favor the correspondence theory.

Before proceeding, I would like to introduce an assumption that will simplify our future reflections considerably. Specifically, I will assume that in addition to being committed to all of the instances of schemas (A), (T), and (AT), we are also committed to the following generalizations:

(A*) ($\Pi p$)(if the state of affairs that $p$ exists, then the state of affairs that $p$ is actual if and only if $p$).

(T*) ($\Pi p$)(the thought that $p$ is true if and only if $p$).

(AT*) ($\Pi p$)(if the state of affairs that $p$ exists, then the thought that $p$ is true if and only if the state of affairs that $p$ is actual).

Also, I will assume that our commitment to (AT*) is in some sense due to our commitment to (A*) and to (T*).

I make no apology for these assumptions, for in my judgment, there are good grounds for thinking that the formal substitutional quantifiers have counterparts in our stock of commonsense logical devices. It stands to reason that if we are committed to all of the instances of (A), (T), and (AT), and we are in possession of logical devices that enable us to express generalizations that summarize those instances, then we are also committed to the generalizations as well. Recognizing, however, that the reader may incline to a different view about the expressive powers of commonsense logic, I hasten to emphasize that I introduce the given assumptions about (A*), (T*), and (AT*) primarily in the interest of simplifying the discussion. Most of what I will say in the sequel can be reformulated in such a way that it depends only on the claim that we are committed to the instances of schemas (A), (T), and (AT).[10,11]

## SECTION VII: CORRESPONDENCE INTUITIONS

We are now in a position to consider the nature and grounds of our correspondence intuitions. We should begin, I think, by considering the following principle, which links truth, semantic correspondence, and actuality:

(CP) For any thought $x$, if there exists a state of affairs $y$ such that $x$ semantically corresponds to $y$, then $x$ is true if and only if there exists a state of affairs $y$ such that $x$ semantically corresponds to $y$ and $y$ is actual.

(CP) seems correct. Since it is concerned with correspondence and truth, the intuition that it is correct counts as a correspondence intuition.

It is possible to explain this intuition by pointing to the following argument:

(SC) For any thought $x$ and any state of affairs $y$, $x$ semantically corresponds to $y$ if and only if ($\Sigma p$)($x$ = the thought that $p$ and $y$ = the state of affairs that $p$).

(AT*) ($\Pi p$)(if the state of affairs that $p$ exists, then the thought that $p$ is true if and only if the state of affairs that $p$ is actual).

---

(CP) For any thought $x$, if there exists a state of affairs $y$ such that $x$ semantically corresponds to $y$, then $x$ is true if and only if there exists a state of affairs $y$ such that $x$ semantically corresponds to $y$ and $y$ is actual.

It is not difficult to see that this argument is valid. Moreover, as has been shown in earlier sections, we are fully committed to (SC) and to (AT*). In view of these facts, it would be surprising if we did not have an intuition that favored (CP).

The foregoing argument provides a proximal explanation of our commitment to (CP), but we can also claim to be in possession of a distal explanation. Thus, in the previous section we took note of this second argument:

(T*) ($\Pi p$)(the thought that $p$ is true if and only if $p$).
(A*) ($\Pi p$)(if the state of affairs that $p$ exists, then the state of affairs that $p$ is actual if and only if $p$).

---

(AT*) ($\Pi p$)(if the state of affairs that $p$ exists, then the thought that $p$ is true if and only if the state of affairs that $p$ is actual).

This argument shows that (AT*) is not a fundamental principle, but rather follows from the deeper principles (T*) and (A*). In view of the argument, we can see that it is possible to obtain a distal explanation of (CP) from the foregoing proximal explanation by replacing (AT*) with deeper principles.

Furthermore, when we reflect on the themes of Chapter 2, we can see that it is possible to construct a third explanation of (CP) – an explanation which represents it as having an even deeper source. In Chapter 2, we observed that there are quite persuasive reasons for thinking that (S) provides an adequate definition of the commonsense concept of truth:

(S) For any $x$, $x$ is true if and only if ($\Sigma p$)(($x =$ the thought that $p$) and $p$).

Now it is possible to construct a derivation leading from (S) to (A*). It follows that we can replace (A*) with (S) in our distal explanation of (CP). This replacement leads to a third explanation of (CP) that runs as follows:

(SC) For any thought $x$ and any state of affairs $y$, $x$ semantically corresponds to $y$ if and only if ($\Sigma p$)($x =$ the thought that $p$ and $y =$ the state of affairs that $p$).

(S) For any $x$, $x$ is true if and only if $(\Sigma p)((x = $ the thought that $p$) and $p$).

(A*) $(\Pi p)$(if the state of affairs that $p$ exists, then the state of affairs that $p$ is actual if and only if $p$).

---

(CP) For any thought $x$, if there exists a state of affairs $y$ such that $x$ semantically corresponds to $y$, then $x$ is true if and only if there exists a state of affairs $y$ such that $x$ semantically corresponds to $y$ and $y$ is actual.

This argument explains our commitment to (CP), and at the same time, it shows that this commitment is absolutely fundamental. It derives (CP) from the *most* basic principle about truth – the principle that serves to define it.[12]

## SECTION VIII: THE CORRESPONDENCE THEORY

We must now consider the question of whether, in addition to the correspondence intuition that is expressed by (CP), there are also correspondence intuitions that show that we are committed to (CT):

(CT) For any thought $x$, $x$ is true if and only if there exists a state of affairs $y$ such that (a) $x$ semantically corresponds to $y$ and (b) $y$ is actual.

Now this is a much stronger proposition than (CP). Thus, unlike (CP), (CT) implies the following existential proposition:

(E) For any thought $x$, if $x$ is true, then there exists a state of affairs $y$ such that $x$ semantically corresponds to $y$.

Accordingly, if it is the case that we are genuinely committed to (CT), it must be the case that (E) is fully in keeping with our semantic and metaphysical intuitions. We can, therefore, investigate the credentials of (CT) by considering whether the latter proposition is genuinely plausible.

I think that, in the end, we are obliged to say that it is not plausible. Thus, consider the class of normative thoughts – the class comprising ethical thoughts, aesthetic thoughts, and such low level commendations and derogations as *mocha ice cream is outtasight* and *mean people suck*. It is far from clear that the members of this class correspond to states of affairs, for it is far from clear that the normative concepts that figure in such thoughts can be said to express or to refer to real properties. On the other hand, it is perfectly clear that we feel entirely comfortable about applying the concept of truth to normative thoughts. Indeed, we often find it essential to do so. Thus, suppose that you feel that you are in possession of evidence that shows that Gandhi was the most enlightened human being, morally speaking, to have ever existed. This view may create a desire to endorse all of Gandhi's views about moral issues. But you may not be in a position to enumerate all of the members of this class of thoughts. In these circumstances, you will find it both natural and necessary to accept the thought that all of the ethical propositions that Gandhi believed are true. Furthermore, you will find it natural and necessary to accept this thought even if you have reservations of the sort just mentioned about the existence of semantic links between ethical thoughts and extraconceptual states of affairs.

It seems to me that situations of this sort arise quite frequently. One wishes to endorse a thought or the members of a class of thoughts – but, for one reason or another, one is unable to entertain the thought or thoughts in question. In other words, one has Quinean reasons for wielding the concept of truth. But it may not be clear to one that the thought or thoughts in question can be said to have *truth conditions* in any thick or full-blooded sense. (One may even be in possession of what one believes to be an unimpeachable argument to the effect that thoughts of the sort in question lack robust truth conditions. For instance, one may be one of the many philosophers who, following Ernest Adams,[13] believe that they have such an argument for a claim to this effect about conditional thoughts.) As I see it, this reluctance to attribute truth conditions is rarely accompanied by a commensurate reluctance to be guided by one's Quinean motives. In situations of the sort under consideration, one insouciantly makes such use of the concept of truth as seems desirable, feeling exactly zero anxiety or remorse about the attendant presuppositions concerning the independence of truth from truth conditions.

In view of these considerations, it seems unlikely that we should be credited with intuitions that indicate the existence of a commitment to (E), and by the same token, it seems unlikely that we should be credited with intuitions that attest to a commitment to (CT). It appears that people who feel that (CT) has direct intuitive appeal are guilty of overgeneralization. It is true, no doubt, that most of the thoughts with which we are concerned in everyday life can be said to have robust truth conditions, or, in other words, to correspond to extraconceptual states of affairs. By the same token, it is no doubt true that in most cases, the thoughts that we hold to be true can be said to have such extraconceptual liaisons. Unless one is careful to keep all of the relevant data in mind, these facts can easily lead one to suppose that (E) and (CT) are fully and explicitly endorsed by intuition. As we have seen, however, this is not a view that is sustained by thorough investigation.

In concluding, I would like to recommend an ecumenical perspective on these matters that I call *extended substitutionalism*. This view endorses the definitions of truth and such other semantic concepts as reference and denotation that are offered by simple substitutionalism. At the same time, however, it acknowledges the existence of a semantic concept that is not recognized by simple substitutionalism, the notion of semantic correspondence, and it also acknowledges the existence of an a priori and necessary link (i.e., (CP)) between this concept and the concept of truth. Thus, while extended substitutionalism does not deny anything that simple substitutionalism affirms, it does make claims that go well beyond those made by simple substitutionalism.

What should we say about the relationship between extended substitutionalism and classical deflationism? It is evident that extended substitutionalism violates certain of the requirements of the latter view, for it invokes the notion of a state of affairs and the notion of actuality, both of which have been viewed by deflationists with hostility and contempt. But should we say that extended substitutionalism represents an abrupt rupture with classical deflationism? Or does it incorporate enough of the elements of deflationism that it is reasonable to describe it as at least quasi-deflationist? I think that it is best to take the latter view. Thus, in the first place, as we just noticed, extended substitutionalism preserves the accounts of truth and a number of other semantic concepts that are offered by simple substitutionalism. These accounts are fully deflationary in both spirit and letter. Second, while it is true that extended substitutionalism explains semantic correspondence in terms of notions that deflationists have found objectionable, it is also true that its account of the semantic relation between thoughts and states of affairs has a genuinely deflationary dimension. This is because extended substitutionalism shows that the apparatus that is needed to characterize that relation of correspondence is significantly less substantial than has traditionally been supposed. It has generally been thought that in order to do justice to our correspondence intuitions, it would be necessary to supplement our theory of thoughts and our theory of states of affairs with a third theory – an independent body of doctrines that focus on correspondence itself. Extended substitutionalism shows that this perception is wrong. It shows that there is no need for a third body of doctrines, for it shows that the mirroring relationship between the realm of thoughts and the realm of states of affairs can be captured by a single definition, a definition that makes use of no concepts other than logical concepts and concepts drawn from the theory of thoughts and the theory of states of affairs. In short, extended substitutionalism presents an account of semantic correspondence that is much more austere than has traditionally been thought possible. By the same token, it shows that the distance separating orthodox deflationists from friends of correspondence is much smaller than has generally been supposed.

In view of these considerations, it seems reasonable to regard extended substitutionalism, not as representing a total departure from classical deflationism, but rather as representing a compromise between classical deflationism and the traditional correspondence theory.

# 4

## *Indexical Representation and Deflationary Semantics*

In the present chapter, I will argue that it is possible to extend deflationary semantic theories in such a way as to explain our use of truth-conditional semantic concepts in connection with indexical concepts and indexical thoughts.

Indexical concepts include *I, you, he, she, it, here, there, now, then, yesterday, two years ago, this rabbit*, and *the table on your left*. They also include all tensed verbal concepts. Indexical thoughts include *I love you, she is having a bad hair day*, and *I used to play tennis with that man*. Roughly speaking, a concept counts as indexical if its reference or denotation depends, at least in part, on features of the *context* in which the concept is entertained. And a thought counts as indexical if it is necessary to take features of the context into account in determining whether the thought counts as true. On the other hand, a concept or a thought counts as *eternal* if its truth-conditional semantic properties are independent of contextual features.

Indexical representations pose a variety of challenging problems for deflationary theories. As I see it, however, it holds quite generally that deflationary theories possess the resources to cope with these problems. That is to say, as I see it, where $D$ is *any* reasonably powerful deflationary theory, it is possible to extend $D$ to a theory that explains the basic features of our semantic thought and talk about indexical representations. I will attempt to establish this generalization by showing that it is satisfied by the simplest and most fundamental form of deflationism, Horwichian minimalism. The explanatory resources of minimalism are very limited – more limited than those of any other reasonably powerful

58

version of deflationism. Accordingly, if it is possible to use minimalism as a foundation for explaining our use of semantic concepts in connection with indexical representations, it must be possible to use any other version of deflationism for the same explanatory ends.

In the present chapter, then, we will be primarily concerned with minimalism, with the result that the substitutional theories of other chapters will not be much in evidence. In Section IX, however, substitutionalism will return to center stage. We will there consider substitutionalism in relation to the problems of indexicality that are discussed earlier in the chapter, and we will seek to determine how exactly substitutionalism should be modified so as to best address these problems.

II

It will be best to begin by taking note of the fact that indexical representations fall into two categories – categories that correspond to different degrees of determinacy or fineness of individuation. These are the category of *determinable indexical representations* and the category of *determinate indexical representations*. This distinction is most easily explained in terms of examples. Suppose that you entertained a thought of the form *I am here now* on the Via Veneto in Rome at midnight on December 31, 1999, and that I entertained a thought of the same form at the same time on Franklin Street in Chapel Hill, North Carolina. There is a sense of "thought" in which it is true to say that you and I entertained the same thought, and also a sense in which it is true to say that you and I entertained different thoughts. When "thought" is used in the first of these senses, it stands for what I wish to call determinable thoughts. Thus, a determinable thought captures what may be common to a highly diverse range of concrete acts of thinking. On the other hand, when "thought" is used in the second of the two senses, it stands for what I wish to call determinate thoughts. Thus, the identities of determinate thoughts are closely linked to the particularities of concrete acts of thinking. Reflection shows that there is a similar distinction to be drawn in the case of concepts.

Determinate representations are individuated by contexts of entertainment. It should not be supposed, however, that they must actually be entertained in order to exist. Thus, for example, there is a determinate thought of the form *I am here now* that I did not entertain, but that I could have entertained if I had been on the Via Veneto at midnight on December 31, 1999. Determinate representations are abstract rather than concrete. They resemble their determinable colleagues in being universals or common natures, though they differ from determinable representations in that their identities are more narrowly circumscribed.

The distinction between determinable representations and determinate representations has not always been recognized in the literature.[1] Accordingly, it may be worth emphasizing that the distinction is honored in our commonsense discourse involving the terms "thought" and "concept." Reflection shows that each of these terms really does have two different senses, corresponding respectively to the distinction between determinable and determinate representations. Thus, consider (1) and (2):

(1) I had the same thought on meeting Tony Blair that Jane had when she first encountered Bill Clinton. We both thought: *This is the most engaging man I have ever met.*
(2) Children begin to acquire such concepts as *here* and *now* early in their second year.

It is evident that these claims are concerned with determinable representations. On the other hand, it is evident that (3) and (4) are concerned with determinate representations:

(3) The thought that you might be willing to marry me is intoxicating.
(4) A thought containing the concept of *this* car will of course have different truth conditions than a thought containing the concept of *that* car.

Reflection shows that it is no less natural and appropriate to make claims like (3) and (4) than to make claims like (1) and (2).

In drawing the distinction between determinable representations and determinate representations, we have taken note of the fact that the class of contexts in which a determinate representation can be entertained is in general highly circumscribed. This fact will turn out to be of fundamental importance in our future inquiries. Accordingly, it seems best to dwell on it a bit, noting several of its facets, and introducing a couple of technical terms that will facilitate our discussion of its implications.

An eternal thought can be entertained in any context. Thus, for example, it would have been possible for Hannibal to have entertained the thought that seven is a prime number while crossing the Alps in 218 B.C., and it would also have been possible for Washington to have entertained it while crossing the Delaware in 1776 A.D. But it is quite otherwise in the case of determinate indexical thoughts. Suppose, for example, that you entertain a thought of the form *I feel witty and pretty and bright*. It is logically impossible for me to entertain the same thought. I can, of course, entertain a thought that has the same form as your thought; but my thought will have a different truth condition, being a thought about me rather than a thought about you. I can also entertain a thought that has the same truth condition as your thought. My thought will not, however, have the same form as your thought, but rather the form *she (or he) feels witty and pretty and bright*. What is impossible is that I entertain a thought that is just like yours in point of form *and* in point of content.

It may be useful to give another example. Suppose again that you entertained a thought of the form *I am here now* while crossing the Via Veneto in Rome at midnight on December 31, 1999. No one other than you could have entertained that thought, nor could you have entertained it at any other place or time.

In general, we can say that determinate representations that have constituents of the form *I* can only be entertained by particular thinkers; that determinate representations that have constituents of the form *here* can only be entertained in particular locations; and that determinate representations that have constituents of the form *now* can only be entertained at particular times. And there are a number of other generalizations of the same sort. Thus, for example, there are a number of generalizations that describe ways in which the entertainability of determinate verbal concepts is restricted or conditioned by the tenses of such concepts.

It will be useful to have a couple of technical terms on hand that can be used to highlight relationships between indexical representations and contexts of the sort we have been considering. If it is logically possible for a determinate representation to be entertained in a context *w*, I will say that the representation is *accessible from w*. And if it is logically impossible for a representation to be entertained in *w*, I will say that it is *inaccessible from w*.

### III

Now that we have distinguished between determinable representations and determinate representations, we are in a position to appreciate a companion distinction between two types of semantic proposition.

First, there are semantic propositions that are concerned with determinable representations. I call them *relational propositions* because the semantic concepts they employ are explicitly or implicitly relational in character, implying that determinable propositions have semantic properties *relative to* contexts of employment. (5) and (6) are two examples:

(5) Where $w$ is any context and $x$ is any agent, the concept *I* refers to $x$ relative to $w$ if and only if $x$ is the agent who counts as the principal thinker in $w$.

(6) Where $w$ is any context, the thought *It is raining here now* is true relative to $w$ if and only if it is raining at the place and time that count respectively as the spatial and temporal coordinates of $w$.

As (5) and (6) indicate, relational propositions presuppose a factoring of contexts into coordinates (or dimensions or components). Every context is seen as having a principal thinker or center of consciousness, a place, a time, a set of objects to which the principal thinker is attending, and so on.

Second, there are semantic propositions that are concerned with determinate representations. Suppose I am currently looking at an older gentleman with whom I am sharing a subway platform. Suppose also that it occurs to me that the gentleman is wearing a magnificent necktie. In these circumstances I might entertain (7):

(7) The thought that the elderly gentleman over there is wearing a magnificent necktie is true.

We can also suppose that, due perhaps to an obsessive theoretical interest in semantic notions, I go on to entertain (8):

(8) When I entertain the thought that the elderly gentleman over there is wearing a magnificent necktie, I am thinking *about* the elderly gentleman over there – that is, I am using a concept that refers to the elderly gentleman.

I will use the expression *absolute proposition* as a term for propositions that resemble (7) and (8) in that they apply semantic notions to determinate representations.

Relational propositions pose problems for theories of semantic notions that are interesting and important. It is plausible, however, that problems of this sort are less fundamental than the problems that are posed by absolute propositions; for it seems that we can explain relational semantic concepts in terms of their absolute counterparts by definitions like the following:

($\star$) Where $x$ is any determinable thought and $w$ is any context, $x$ is true relative to $w$ if and only if there is a determinate thought $z$ such that (a) $z$ is accessible from $w$, (b) $z$ is true (in the absolute sense), and (c) $z$ is a "particularization" of $x$, in the sense that $z$ has the same logical form as $x$, contains exactly the same nonindexical conceptual constituents as $x$, and contains determinate indexicals that count as determinate forms of the determinable concepts that figure in $x$.

At all events, I will assume here that definitions like (⋆) are correct.[2] Correlatively, I will assume that it is appropriate to set questions about relational propositions aside, and to focus exclusively on questions about absolute propositions.

Continuing now with our taxonomic efforts, let us take note of an important distinction within the category of absolute propositions. Some members of this category are *intracontextual* while others are *intercontextual*.

Where $P$ is an absolute proposition, I will say that $P$ is intracontextual if and only if there is a context $w$ such that (a) $P$ is accessible from $w$ and (b) the representation (or representations) with which $P$ is concerned is (are) also accessible from $w$.

Returning to the example of the elderly subway traveler, recall that both (7) and (8) are concerned with a determinate representation that is deployable (and is in fact actually deployed) on the occasion on which I am deploying (7) and (8) themselves. Because of this fact, they both count as intracontextual representations.

When I speak of intercontextual propositions, on the other hand, I will mean to refer to semantic propositions that differ from their intracontextual colleagues precisely in that they are concerned with propositions that are *not* accessible from some of the contexts from which they are themselves accessible.

Continuing with our running example, suppose that our elderly friend takes notice of me as I examine his tie and is moved to address me as follows:

(9) Sir! It is evident that you are envious of my necktie!

Here it is natural for me to infer that the gentleman is using (9) to express an indexical thought – a thought that has the following form:

(10) The fellow who is staring at me is envious of my necktie.

Now I cannot myself entertain the determinate thought that my fellow traveler is entertaining; for if I were to entertain a thought of form (10), it would be quite different in subject matter than the thought that the elderly gentleman is expressing. (It would be a thought about the elderly gentleman and *my* necktie.) Thus, the determinate thought that the elderly gentleman is expressing by (9) is inaccessible to me. But I may still use an absolute thought to ascribe truth to the elderly gentleman's thought.

Suppose that I do formulate a thought of this sort. Suppose in particular that I formulate a thought that is of form (11):

(11) The thought that the elderly gentleman expressed by his remark is true.

In entertaining this last thought, I am entertaining a paradigmatic inter-contextual proposition.

IV

As we observed in Section I, the purpose of the present chapter is to show that it is possible to extend deflationary semantic theories so as to explain the main facts concerning our use of semantic concepts in connection with indexical representations. Thus far, I have been mainly concerned with introducing the relevant facts and taxonomizing them. I will now review the main features of a particularly simple deflationary theory – the theory that Paul Horwich has recommended under the name *minimalism*. The conceptual framework of minimalism is more austere than that of any other version of deflationism. Accordingly, if it is possible to extend minimalism so as to explain the main facts concerning the semantic properties of indexical representations, it must be possible to achieve similar results with all other deflationary theories.

Now in the *locus classicus* of minimalism, Horwich's book on truth,[3] there is very little explicit discussion of indexicals of any kind, and such discussion as there is appears to focus on the semantic notions we use in connection with *linguistic* indexicals – that is, in connection with indexical words and indexical sentences. In view of these facts, whatever Horwich's intentions may have been, I propose here to construe Horwichian minimalism as concerned exclusively with the semantic notions that we use in connection with *eternal* representations. After expounding Horwichian minimalism in the present section, I will go on to seek a more inclusive minimalism. That is to say, I will try to construct a theory that incorporates Horwich's views about propositions that ascribe semantic concepts to eternal representations, but that offers an account of the semantic concepts that we use in connection with indexical representations as well. In framing the latter part of the theory, I will attempt to formulate proposals that are as similar as possible in spirit to the Horwichian proposals in the former part.

As we saw in Chapter 1, Horwich explains the notion of truth that we apply to eternal thoughts by saying that it is implicitly defined by the class of thoughts that have form (T):

(T) The thought that $p$ is true if and only if $p$.

He offers a similar account of the notion of satisfaction (or, as I will say, denotation) that we use in connection with eternal general concepts, claiming that it is implicitly defined by the class of all thoughts that are substitution instances of (D):

(D) For all $x$, the concept of an $F$ denotes $x$ if and only if $x$ is an $F$.

Horwich also provides a closely related account of the notion of reference that we use in connection with eternal singular concepts. Thus, he tells us that this notion is defined by the instances of schema (R):

(R) For all $x$, the concept of $a$ refers to $x$ if and only if $x$ is identical with $a$.

It is clear that (T), (D), and (R) exemplify a common pattern. Horwich claims that this pattern holds across the board. That is to say, he claims that all of the semantic notions that we use in connection with eternal representations can be explained in terms of schemas like (T), (D), and (R).

A theory of truth must explain what it is for an agent to possess the concept of truth. Horwich provides the germ of such an account, claiming, in effect, that an agent possesses the concept of truth if and only if the agent is disposed to accept, without evidence, any thought that is an instance of schema (T).[4] This is helpful, but it fails to honor the complexity of a couple of important issues. Accordingly, I propose to understand minimalism as incorporating the following more elaborate possession condition:

(PC) Where $x$ is any agent, $x$ possesses the concept of truth if and only if $x$ satisfies the following three conditions: (1) for every thought $y$ that is constructible using concepts that are components of $x$'s actual conceptual scheme, $x$ is disposed to accept, without empirical evidence and without supporting a priori argumentation, the instance of (T) that is concerned with $y$; (2) for every conceptual scheme $C$ such that (a) $C$ can be obtained by modifications of $x$'s actual conceptual scheme, and (b) it is in principle possible for $x$ to grasp all of the component concepts of $C$, it is true that if $x$ possessed $C$ instead of his or her actual conceptual scheme, then, for every thought $y$ that is constructible using components of $C$, $x$ would be disposed to accept, without empirical evidence and without supporting a priori argumentation, the instance of (T) that is concerned with $y$; and (3) apart from obvious laws of logic, there are no propositions involving the concept of truth other than propositions of form (T) that $x$ is disposed to accept without empirical evidence and without supporting a priori argumentation.

This proposal resembles Horwich's proposal in being based on the idea that possession of the concept of truth involves being disposed to accept instances of schema (T) without evidence, but it differs from Horwich's proposal in that it does not carry the suggestion that an agent must be disposed to accept *every* such instance in order to possess the concept. It is, I think, important to avoid this suggestion. Our intuitions tell us that the average human agent is in full possession of the concept of truth. It seems most unlikely, however, that the average human agent is disposed to accept every instance of schema (T). After all, it is highly plausible that there are instances of (T) whose constituent concepts lie beyond the cognitive capacities of human agents.

Although (PC) does not require that an agent stand in a separate cognitive relation to each instance of schema (T), it nonetheless makes a quite substantial demand, requiring that agents possess cognitive capacities that enable them to track the *form* represented by schema (T) across a variety of divergent conceptual schemes. This requirement can only be satisfied by agents who can be credited with a full cognitive grasp of that form, a grasp that is not colored or conditioned in any way by considerations having to do with conceptual content.

I wish to claim, then, that (PC) is more liberal than Horwich's proposal, in that it allows agents with limited conceptual capacities to possess the concept of truth, and also that (PC) is nonetheless quite demanding, in that it calls for cognitive resources that are powerful enough to separate the form that is captured by schema (T) from any commonalities of content that might be possessed by sets of instances of that form. I also wish to claim that these features of (PC) are significant virtues, enabling it to honor deep-seated intuitions about the way in which possession of the concept of truth is distributed across the space of actual and imaginary agents.

There is, however, one respect in which (PC) is less than fully satisfactory. To obtain a fully satisfactory possession condition, it is necessary to supplement (PC) with instructions for interpreting a couple of its constituent quantifiers.

Part (1) of (PC) contains the quantifier "for every thought $y$ that is constructible using concepts that are components of $x$'s actual conceptual scheme," and part (2) contains the quantifier "for every thought $y$ that is constructible using components of $C$ (where $C$ is an alternative to $x$'s actual conceptual scheme)." In each case, the quantifier should be understood as having restricted range, involving only those thoughts that are sufficiently short that it is in principle possible for the relevant agent *x* to entertain them. Thus, for example, the first quantifier should be understood as an abbreviation for "for every thought *y* such that (a) *y* is constructible using only concepts that are components of *x*'s actual conceptual scheme and (b) *y* is sufficiently short that it is in principle possible for *x* to entertain *y*." Unless they are understood to be governed by restrictions like (b), the two quantifiers would make it impossible for human agents to possess the concept of truth. Thus, where *C* is any conceptual scheme that a human agent is likely to employ, *C* will involve recursive devices that are capable of generating thoughts of arbitrary length. But it is plausible that there is an upper bound on the lengths of thoughts that human agents are capable of entertaining.

In addition to explaining what it is for an agent to possess the concept of truth, a theory of truth should explain what is involved when an agent grasps what it is for a particular thought to be true. Minimalism can easily be extended in such a way as to fulfill this second obligation. Thus, it is natural to supplement the claims we have considered thus far with the following closely related claim:

(G) For every agent *x* and every thought *y*, *x* grasps what it is for *y* to be true if and only if *x* understands and accepts the instance of (T) that is concerned with *y*.

Eventually, after we have enlarged the scope of our concerns to include indexical thoughts, we will find reason to qualify (G). But (G) appears to offer a perfectly satisfactory account of what it is to grasp the truth condition of an eternal proposition.

I have been arguing, in effect, that it is desirable to modify Horwichian minimalism by augmenting it with (PC) and (G). When these changes are combined with a few others that are closely related, we arrive at a theory that I will call *augmented Horwichian minimalism* (*AHM*). This theory has three main components. First, there is the claim that the truth–conditional semantic concepts we use in connection with eternal representations owe their contents to implicit definitions involving propositions that are instances of schemas like (T), (D), and (R). The second component is a set of principles that contains (PC) and also several similar propositions that formulate possession conditions for truth-conditional semantic notions other than truth. The third component is a set of principles that contains (G) and also several similar propositions about what it is to grasp facts about the reference and denotation of particular eternal concepts.

Before going on to consider how to extend AHM to an account of the semantic notions we apply to indexical representations, I would like to pause to consider a consequence of AHM that is mildly counterintuitive. The consequence I have in mind may be formulated as follows:

(C) It is possible to possess the concept of truth without grasping, and without even being disposed to grasp, all of the propositions that play a role in fixing the content of the concept.

To appreciate that (C) really does follow from AHM, it is sufficient to note two facts. In the first place, AHM claims that *every* proposition of form (T) plays a role in fixing the content of the concept of truth. It follows from this claim that if any one such proposition were somehow taken away, the content of the concept of truth would be different, albeit only to a small degree. Second, AHM claims that the requirement given in (PC) is a sufficient condition for possessing the concept of truth. In view of the foregoing comments about the proper interpretation of the quantifiers in (PC), it is clear that it is possible for an agent $x$ to satisfy the requirement in question without being disposed to accept every instance of (T). It is enough that $x$ be disposed to accept all of the propositions of form (T) that meet the following two rather stringent conditions: (a) they are of such a length as to be surveyable by $x$; and (b) they are constructible using the resources of a conceptual scheme that it would be in principle possible for $x$ to acquire.

As noted, the indicated consequence of AHM is mildly counterintuitive. Apparently, we have intuitions that seem to us to favor the following *intimacy principle*:

If a class of propositions constitutes the correct definition of a concept, then, in order to possess the concept, an agent must stand in an intimate cognitive relationship to each individual proposition in the class.

This principle enjoys a certain amount of prima facie plausibility, for it holds in a large range of cases – specifically, in all those cases in which the components of a complex definition *lack* a common form. In my view, however, its plausibility is specious: there is good reason to doubt that it holds in all cases.

When the component clauses of a definition are formally disparate, it is clear that an agent must stand in an intimate cognitive relation to each clause in order to count as being *en rapport* with the whole definition. Reflection indicates, however, that when the components of a definition have a common form, it is enough that an agent have dispositions that make it appropriate to say that the agent is cognitively linked to the form.

The agent's relationship to the form is sufficient to induce an indirect relationship to the individual propositions that count as instances of the form.[5]

One way to appreciate this is to observe that there are clear counterexamples to the foregoing intimacy principle. Consider, for example, the first order concept of natural number. The set of propositions that implicitly define this concept is infinite, since it includes infinitely many propositions that are instances of the following induction schema:

If it is the case (a) that 0 is $F$ and (b) that for each natural number $n$, if $n$ is $F$ then $n + 1$ is $F$, then it is also the case that every natural number is $F$.

Now propositions of this form can be of arbitrary complexity, and it is therefore impossible for a human agent to entertain them all. Even so, however, we feel entirely comfortable about attributing the first order concept of natural number to human agents. Here, then, we have an example showing that the foregoing intimacy principle is too strong. There are a number of other counterexamples of the same sort, including the first order concept of identity and the ZF concept of a set.

The intimacy principle is also called into question by considerations having to do with our elementary logical concepts. Consider, for example, the following schematic inference:

It is not the case that it is not the case that $p$
_____
$p$

It is plausible that the concept of classical negation is partially defined by inferences that have this form. Moreover, it is plausible that every such inference counts as a component of the definition. But inferences of the form in question can contain propositions of arbitrary complexity. Moreover, in many cases, their constituent concepts include concepts that lie altogether outside the ken of human agents. Yet it is clear that we are fully prepared to attribute the concept of classical negation to virtually the entire family of human agents.[6]

It turns out, then, that in addition to being beautifully simple and having a number of other intrinsic virtues, AHM can be defended against certain intuitions that appear to call it into question. AHM is an attractive and resilient theory. This is not to say that it does justice to all of the relevant data. Indeed, as an advocate of substitutionalism, I am committed to denying that it does. At the same time, however, I think that the virtues of AHM give us reason to believe that it is similar in spirit, and even to a certain extent in letter, to more adequate accounts of truth.

Assuming that this is correct, if we make use of AHM as a guide in constructing a theory of the semantic notions that we apply to *indexical* representations, we can reasonably hope that we will not go too badly astray.


V

Our task is now to consider whether, and if so, how, it is possible to extend AHM so that it applies to absolute semantic propositions – that is, to semantic propositions that are concerned with determinate indexical representations. As a first step, I will generalize AHM in what appears to be the simplest and most natural way. It will be felt, I think, that the resulting theory, which I will call *simple extended minimalism* (*SEM*), has some important virtues. In order to obtain a fully satisfactory account, however, it will prove necessary to modify one component of SEM, and to supplement SEM with some additional explanatory apparatus. I will attempt to provide the necessary improvements and supplements in the next section.

SEM is very similar to AHM. The principal difference is that it involves a broader understanding of what is to count as an instance of schema (T):

(T) The thought that $p$ is true if and only if $p$.

Up to this point, we have been concerned exclusively with thoughts that can be obtained from (T) by replacing the schematic thought $p$ with eternal thoughts. SEM joins AHM in recognizing all of these thoughts as instances of schema (T), but it also takes the class of instances of (T) to include the thoughts that can be obtained by replacing $p$ with determinate indexical thoughts. Thus, for example, every determinate thought of form (13) will count as an instance of (T):

(13) The thought that I am here now is true if and only if I am here now.

SEM has a similarly broad understanding of what is to count as an instance of schema (D), and also of what is to count as an instance of schema (R). And in general, its claims about semantic concepts other than truth are similar to its claims about truth. In view of these similarities, it will be possible in the sequel to set the claims about other semantic concepts aside and to focus on the claims about truth. Our conclusions about the latter claims will generalize smoothly to conclusions about all of the main components of SEM.

Having broadened the notion of an instance of (T), SEM goes on to assert that the concept of truth is implicitly defined by the class of thoughts that fall under this notion. Thus, according to SEM, instances of (13) are components of a correct definition of truth.

Further, SEM explains what it is to possess the concept of truth in terms of a principle that is formally identical to the possession condition that figures in AHM:

(PC⋆) Where $x$ is any agent, $x$ possesses the concept of truth if and only if $x$ satisfies the following three conditions: (1) for every thought $y$ that is constructible using concepts that are components of $x$'s actual conceptual scheme, $x$ is disposed to accept, without evidence and without supporting a priori argumentation, the instance of (T) that is concerned with $y$; (2) for every conceptual scheme $C$ such that (a) $C$ can be obtained by modifications of $x$'s actual conceptual scheme, and (b) it is in principle possible for $x$ to grasp all of the component concepts of $C$, it is true that if $x$ possessed $C$ instead of his or her actual conceptual scheme, then, for every thought $y$ that is constructible using components of $C$, $x$ would be disposed to accept, without empirical evidence and without supporting a priori argumentation, the instance of (T) that is concerned with $y$; and (3) apart from obvious laws of logic, there are no propositions involving the concept of truth other than propositions of form (T) that $x$ is disposed to accept without empirical evidence and without supporting a priori argumentation.

There is just one difference between this principle and its predecessor: In (PC⋆), "instance of (T)" is to be understood as denoting instances involving determinate indexical thoughts as well as instances involving eternal thoughts.

(An aside: When we initially encountered principle (PC), we agreed to construe its two quantifiers beginning "for every thought $y$" as being governed by an implicit restriction, a restriction that in effect limits their scope to thoughts that are of moderate length. We should view the corresponding quantifiers in (PC⋆) as governed by a similar restriction.)

Finally, SEM puts forward the following counterpart of principle (G):

(G⋆) For every agent $x$ and every thought $y$, $x$ grasps what it is for $y$ to be true if and only if $x$ understands and accepts the instance of (T) that is concerned with $y$.

The relationship between (G⋆) and (G) is the same as the relationship between (PC⋆) and (PC): (G⋆) differs from (G) only in that it involves an appropriately broadened understanding of what is to count as an instance of schema (T).

Now SEM has a consequence that can appear, at least prima facie, to run counter to our intuitions. This consequence is similar to the prima facie counterintuitive consequence that we considered in the previous section. There is a difference, however, and this difference might be thought to make the present consequence much less tractable than the one we considered earlier.

To appreciate the consequence I have in mind here, recall our earlier distinction between accessible and inaccessible indexical thoughts. A thought is inaccessible from a context if it is logically possible for the thought to be entertained in the context. Otherwise the thought is inaccessible from the context. The consequence I have in mind comes to the fore when we consider SEM in relation to this distinction.

So as to fix ideas, let us focus on a particular context $C$ and a particular indexical thought $I$ that is inaccessible from $C$. Let $TI$ be the instance of schema (T) that is concerned with $I$. Now $I$ is a constituent of $TI$, so $I$'s being inaccessible from $C$ implies that $TI$ is inaccessible from $C$. Thus, if Jones is the agent who counts as the principal thinker in $C$, it is logically impossible for Jones to entertain $TI$. But still, despite this inability on Jones's part, SEM allows Jones to possess the concept of truth. For (PC★) does not require that an agent be disposed to accept all instances of schema (T). Rather it requires only that an agent be disposed to accept all those instances of (T) that it is possible for the agent to entertain. Thus, SEM implies both that the thought $TI$ plays an essential role in fixing the content of the concept of truth and that it is logically possible for an agent who is logically barred from entertaining $TI$ to count as being in full possession of the concept.

Let us compare this situation with the situation that we encountered in the previous section. In Section IV, we found that AHM implies the following proposition: It is logically possible for an agent to be in full possession of the concept of truth even though there are essential components of the definition of the concept which, *as a matter of actual fact*, the agent is not disposed to accept. We have now found that SEM entails this rather different proposition: It is logically possible for an agent to be in full possession of the concept of truth even though there are essential components of the definition of the concept that *it is logically impossible* for the agent to accept. Now it seems correct to say that each of these propositions is counterintuitive, but it also seems correct to say that the first is less counterintuitive than the second. Accordingly, someone who felt that it is possible to deal successfully with the problem for AHM that is posed by the first proposition might still despair of coping with the problem for SEM that is posed by the second problem.

My own feeling, however, is that the considerations that we found to neutralize the first problem apply also with equal force to the second. In considering the first problem, we observed that an agent who satisfies the requirement given in (PC) can reasonably be held to stand in an intimate cognitive relation to the *form* that is shared by the eternal instances of (T), and that this fact provides a ground for saying that the agent also stands in a cognitive relation, albeit a less intimate one, to the various particular instances. It seems to me that essentially the same thing can be said about the requirement given in (PC$\star$) and the enlarged class of instances of (T) with which (PC$\star$) is concerned. An agent who satisfies the requirement given in (PC$\star$) can reasonably be held to stand in an intimate cognitive relation to the form that is represented by schema (T). Accordingly, if an agent satisfies the requirement given in (PC$\star$), it seems fair to say that he or she stands in an indirect cognitive relation to the whole range of instances of (T), inaccessible instances as well as accessible ones.

In considering these matters, it may be helpful to reflect anew on the situation involving logical concepts like negation and disjunction. It is a commonplace that the content of the concept of disjunction is partially determined by instances of *Disjunction Introduction*:

$$ \text{(DI1)} \quad \frac{p}{p \text{ or } q} \qquad \text{(DI2)} \quad \frac{q}{p \text{ or } q} $$

Accordingly, if an agent possesses the concept of disjunction, then he or she must do so in virtue of standing in some sort of cognitive relation to the concrete inferences that count as instances of (DI1) or (DI2). Reflection shows, however, that for any agent $x$, there will be an indefinitely large class of inferences of the form (DI1) and an indefinitely large class of form (DI2) that are inaccessible to $x$. (For Disjunction Introduction may be performed with indexical thoughts as well as eternal ones.) Accordingly, unless we are to conclude that no human agent can possess the concept of disjunction, we must say that agents can possess the concept in virtue of relations to the instances of (DI1) and to the instances of (DI2) that are weak and highly attenuated, being mediated by a cognitive relation to the forms of inference represented by (DI1) and (DI2) themselves. I would like to suggest that in addition to being inevitable, the latter claim also seems, after careful consideration, to be entirely natural and appropriate. And in addition, I would like to suggest that the corresponding claim about the concept of truth can come to seem entirely natural and appropriate as well.

VI

I wish to turn now to consider a worry about SEM of a quite different nature. This worry is prompted by the following question: Is SEM compatible with an acceptable account of our *knowledge* of intercontextual propositions? It is not immediately clear how this question is to be answered, but there are grounds for concern that the answer will turn out to be negative. Thus, it can appear that any acceptable account of our knowledge of truth-ascriptions will entail the claims made in the following paragraph:

(P) We are often concerned to arrive at a semantic assessment of a thought that is being entertained, or that could be entertained, by a thinker in a different context. Sometimes we arrive at such assessments by inferring them from generalizations. (Thus, for example, I may arrive at the conclusion that the thought expressed by Gordon's most recent remark is true by inferring it from two other propositions – the proposition that the thought expressed by Gordon's most recent remark was concerned with complexity theory, and the proposition that all of Gordon's beliefs about complexity theory are true.) But when we are concerned to assess a thought directly, without considering it in relation to generalizations, we must make explicit use of a grasp of what it is for that particular thought to be true, that is, a grasp of the truth condition of the thought. This is no less true in the case of indexical thoughts than in the case of eternal thoughts. Moreover, it holds for both varieties of indexical thoughts – those that are accessible from the context of assessment and those that are inaccessible from that context.

Now (P) is irreconcilably at odds with SEM. Thus, SEM entails that our grasp of what it is for a thought to be true (i.e., our knowledge of the truth condition of the thought) consists in acceptance of the instance of schema (T) that is concerned with that thought. It follows that if we were to accept both (P) and SEM, we would become committed to the proposition that it is impossible for us to arrive at defensible semantic evaluations of inaccessible thoughts. This proposition is clearly at variance with the facts. Thus, for example, it is evident that I can have good reason to hold that you are currently entertaining a thought of the form *I am holding a truly outstanding blueberry muffin in my left hand*, and it is no less evident that I can have good reason to hold that your thought is true.

It is clear, then, that there are grounds for thinking that SEM is called into question by considerations having to do with our knowledge of intercontextual propositions. This is, I think, the main difficulty confronting SEM. I will call it the *problem of intercontextual knowledge.*

In the next section, I will attempt to show that SEM can survive this difficulty. My defense will be based on a proposal for modifying SEM, and also on an account of the inferential processes that underlie our intercontextual semantic assessments.

VII

In order to meet the problem of intercontextual knowledge, it is necessary, I believe, to revise SEM by liberalizing its account of what it is to grasp the truth condition of a thought. The liberalization I have in mind derives from the observation that there are two ways in which an agent can grasp a truth condition. First, there is *direct* grasping. One directly grasps the truth condition of a thought $y$ when one understands and accepts the instance of schema (T) that is concerned with $y$ – that is, when one satisfies the condition that figures in definition (G⋆). Second, there is *indirect* grasping. Suppose that you entertained a thought of the form *I feel witty tonight* at midnight, December 31, 1999, and suppose also that I was concerned to grasp the truth condition of your thought at some point during the morning of the next day. Even though I was unable to entertain the very same thought that you had entertained, it was within my power to entertain a certain *translation* of your thought. Specifically, it was within my power to entertain a thought which has the form *she (or he) felt witty last night* and which contains determinate concepts that refer respectively to you and to the night of the 31st. Suppose that I did in fact entertain the latter thought. And finally, suppose that the following two conditions were satisfied: First, I believed that the second thought was a good translation of your thought; and second, I understood and accepted the instance of schema (T) that is concerned with the second thought. Given these assumptions, it is reasonable to say, I believe, that I *indirectly* grasped the truth condition of your thought. And in general, it is reasonable to say that an agent indirectly grasps the truth condition of an inaccessible thought $y$ if the agent directly grasps the truth condition of an accessible thought that the agent correctly believes to be a good translation of the first thought.

I wish to propose, then, that we revise SEM by replacing (G*) with the following two definitions:

(G**) For any agent $x$ and any thought $y$, $x$ *directly grasps* what it is for $y$ to be true if and only if $x$ understands and accepts the instance of (T) that is concerned with $y$.

(IG) For any agent $x$ and any thought $y$, $x$ *indirectly grasps* what it is for $y$ to be true if and only if there is a thought $z$ such that (a) $x$ directly grasps what it is for $z$ to be true, (b) $x$ is disposed to believe, and would be justified in believing, that $z$ is a good translation of $y$, and (c) it is in fact true that $z$ is a good translation of $y$.[7]

Furthermore, I wish to suggest that the relevant notion of a good translation is captured by the following definition:

(TR) For any two thoughts $y$ and $z$, $z$ is a *good translation* of $y$ if and only if $z$ and $y$ satisfy the following four conditions: (a) some of the indexical concepts in $z$ are different than the corresponding indexical concepts in $y$; (b) despite these differences, each referring concept in $z$ is coreferential with its counterpart in $y$; (c) necessarily, $z$ and $y$ have the same truth value; and (d) there are no differences between $y$ and $z$ beyond the ones noted in (a).

Here, of course, the relevant notions of reference and truth are the ones that are made available by SEM.

This proposal is appealing; but before we can embrace it, we must consider whether it is in keeping with the pertinent psychological facts. Do agents normally have the abilities that are presupposed by the definition of indirect grasping? That is to say, is it within the power of normal agents, at least in cases in which they count intuitively as grasping the truth conditions of inaccessible thoughts, to construct good translations of those thoughts? Unless the answer to this question is affirmative, the present account of indirect grasping does not represent a correct solution to the problem of intercontextual knowledge.

There is also an epistemological issue that we must address. In order to satisfy the requirements of the definition of indirect grasping, it is not enough that an agent construct a counterpart of an inaccessible thought that counts as a good translation of the thought. It must also be the case that the agent is *justified in believing* that the counterpart is a good translation. So we must ask: do agents normally satisfy this epistemological requirement? Do they normally have good reason to believe that constructed counterparts of inaccessible thoughts are good translations? Again, it is necessary to show that the answer is affirmative before the present proposal can be deemed adequate.

Taking the psychological question first, let us begin by observing that every normal human agent has the capacity to interpret indexical assertions in his or her native language. Thus, for example, suppose that a certain speaker of English, Jones, receives a message containing the following indexical assertions:

(16) I am having a bad hair day today.
(17) The man who sat next to me on the subway this morning was wearing a magnificent necktie.
(18) It has been raining here for two days.

Suppose also that Jones receives this message the day after it was composed, and that Jones is aware of this relationship between the time of composition and the time of arrival. Suppose finally that Jones is aware that the author of the message was a male. In these circumstances, Jones will automatically come to believe the following thoughts:

(19) He asserted that he was having a bad hair day yesterday.
(20) He asserted that the man who was sitting next to him on the subway yesterday morning was wearing a magnificent necktie.
(21) He asserted that it had been raining in the place where he was located for two days.

Let us say that (19)–(21) contain *interpretive counterparts* of the thoughts that are expressed by (16)–(18). Described in general terms, the ability to produce such counterparts is the ability to move from information about the intrinsic natures of indexical assertions and information about their contexts to certain accessible thoughts – specifically, to accessible thoughts that closely resemble the inaccessible thoughts that the assertions express. It is clear that this ability is very powerful: anyone who possesses it is in a position to interpret indexical assertions of a large range of lengths and complexities. It is also clear that the ability is quite common, being part of the standard equipment of any competent speaker of a natural language.[8]

Reflection shows that we rely heavily on interpretive counterparts in assessing the thoughts of others for truth value, and also in determining what objects and properties the thoughts of others are about. Suppose that Jones judges that the thought expressed by (16) in the foregoing example is true. It is plausible that if Jones were asked to express his reason for making this judgment in full detail, he would say something like the following: "Well, the writer used the sentence to express the thought that he was having a bad hair day yesterday; and that thought is true if he was in fact having a bad hair day yesterday. Now in my experience the hair of the individual in question is almost always a mess. Hence, it is very likely that the thought is true." Further, suppose Jones judges that the thought expressed by (16) is about April 15, 2000. If asked for his rationale for this second judgment, he would very likely say something like "Well, the thought is clearly about yesterday, and yesterday was April 15, 2000." In each of these cases, Jones is basing a semantic judgment about a target thought on a semantic judgment about his interpretive counterpart of that thought. He is, in effect, projecting a semantic property of his interpretive thought onto the target thought. Reflection suggests that use of this procedure is the norm.

We also rely heavily on interpretive counterparts in attributing propositional attitudes to other agents. Suppose that Jon asserts the sentence "I will be obliged to vote for Ralph Nader in the next election," and suppose also that my interpretive counterpart of the thought that is expressed by this assertion is a thought of the form *he will be obliged for Ralph Nader in the next election*. Suppose also that I wish to frame a thought which represents Jon as believing the thought that he expresses by the sentence. Here I will make use of my interpretive counterpart of his thought, framing a thought of the form *he believes that he will be obliged to vote for Ralph Nader in the next election*. In doing so, I will do what is typically done. In general, we feel that it is both possible and necessary to make use of interpretive counterparts in reporting beliefs.[9]

In addition to possessing an ability to produce interpretive counterparts of thoughts that are expressed linguistically, we also have an ability to produce counterparts of thoughts that are expressed by nonlinguistic behavior. Thus, for example, suppose that Jay sees Kate holding a blueberry muffin in her left hand, and that he observes that she is regarding it with appreciation and gustatory anticipation. In this case, if Jay wishes to attribute an appropriate belief to Kate, he will frame a thought of the form *she believes that she is holding a delicious blueberry muffin in her left hand*. Thus, in attributing the belief to Kate, Jay will be making use of a thought that is formally distinct from the thought that is the true object of her belief (for presumably the true object is a thought of the form *I am holding a delicious blueberry muffin in my left hand*), but it will resemble her thought in the same way that interpretive counterparts were seen to resemble target thoughts in the foregoing examples involving linguistic behavior.

To summarize these observations, we have found that human agents are normally in possession of abilities that enable them to frame accessible counterparts of inaccessible thoughts. It appears that we rely heavily on such counterparts in arriving at conclusions about the semantic properties of inaccessible thoughts, and that we also rely heavily on them in constructing descriptions of propositional attitudes that have inaccessible thoughts as their objects.

VIII

We embarked on our current investigative path because we were interested in the question of whether human agents normally possess psychological abilities that make it possible for them to satisfy the requirements of (IG):

(IG) For any agent $x$ and any thought $y$, $x$ *indirectly grasps* what it is for $y$ to be true if and only if there is a thought $z$ such that (a) $x$ directly grasps what it is for $z$ to be true, (b) $x$ is disposed to believe, and would be justified in believing, that $z$ is a good translation of $y$, and (c) it is in fact true that $z$ is a good translation of $y$.

We can now say that the answer to the question appears to be affirmative. Thus, we have found that human agents are capable of constructing counterparts of the inaccessible thoughts of their fellow agents. Moreover, when one reflects on examples like the ones presented above, one comes naturally to the conclusion that the counterparts in question are normally such as to count as good translations of the thoughts that they represent. Bringing these observations together, we arrive at the view that human agents are normally equipped with abilities that enable them to satisfy the requirements of (IG). But more: we have found that agents normally make use of these abilities in forming opinions about the truth values of inaccessible thoughts. It follows from this that we use the abilities in question in grasping what it is for inaccessible thoughts to be true, that is, in grasping the truth conditions of such thoughts. This additional finding indicates that our proposed solution to the problem of intercontextual knowledge is fully in accord with the relevant psychological facts.

As the reader will recall, however, there is also a pressing epistemological question about (IG). It may be intuitively natural to suppose that our interpretive abilities enable us to produce counterparts of inaccessible thoughts that count as good translations of those thoughts, but is this supposition fully defensible? Are there good reasons for embracing it? And, what is most to the point, is it plausible that normal human agents are in possession of such reasons? That is to say, is it plausible that human agents are normally in a position to satisfy part (b) of (IG)? We must now consider this question about part (b). (Of course, if it is possible to show that agents normally satisfy (b), it will follow that we, as theorists of interpretation, are in possession of good reasons to think that part (c) of (IG) is normally satisfied. Thus, if we can show that (b) is normally satisfied, we will be done. There will be no need to conduct a separate investigation concerning part (c).)

To fix ideas, we should remind ourselves that we are working with a notion of good translation that is defined as follows:

(TR) For any two thoughts $y$ and $z$, $z$ is a *good translation* of $y$ if and only if $z$ and $y$ satisfy the following four conditions: (a) some of the indexical concepts in $z$ are different than the corresponding indexical concepts in $y$; (b) despite these differences, each referring concept in $z$ is coreferential with its counterpart in $y$; (c) necessarily, $z$ and $y$ have the same truth value; and (d) there are no differences between $y$ and $z$ beyond the ones noted in (a).

Thus, our present task is to determine whether agents can know that interpretive counterparts are normally such as to satisfy conditions (a)–(d).

In considering this issue, we should begin by observing that the use that we make of interpretive counterparts presupposes that they satisfy the conditions in question. Thus, as we saw, we rely on interpretive counterparts in forming judgments about the truth values and aboutness-properties of inaccessible thoughts, and in framing descriptions of propositional attitudes that have inaccessible thoughts as their objects. It is easily seen that these practices commit us to the proposition that interpretive counterparts are good translations of the thoughts we use to represent them. Thus, it would clearly be inappropriate for me to derive a conclusion about the truth value of one of your thoughts from a perception concerning the truth value of one of my thoughts unless I was prepared to adopt the view that the two thoughts have the same truth value. (Here we should note that I tend to arrive at conclusions to the effect that certain of your thoughts are *necessarily* true by deriving them from propositions to the effect that my corresponding thoughts are necessarily true. It would be inappropriate for me to proceed in this way unless I was prepared to adopt the view that my interpretive counterparts of your thoughts are necessarily the same in point of truth value.) Further, it would clearly be inappropriate for me to derive conclusions concerning the aboutness-properties of your thoughts from perceptions concerning the aboutness-properties of corresponding thoughts of my own unless I was disposed to judge that corresponding constituents of our thoughts tend to coincide in reference.

And, finally, it would clearly be inappropriate for me to make use of my thoughts in framing descriptions of your propositional attitudes unless I was disposed to judge that your thoughts are as similar as possible to mine in point of form. (Observe here that I infer conclusions about the logical consequences of your attitudes from my descriptions of your attitudes. It would clearly be inappropriate for me to proceed in this way unless I was disposed to judge that the thoughts that figure in my descriptions closely resemble the thoughts that serve as the objects of your attitudes in point of form.)

It appears, then, that we have several practices that, collectively, at least, commit us to the view that interpretive counterparts of inaccessible thoughts are good translations of the thoughts to which they correspond. My next point is that the practices in question have enormous predictive value. This is easily seen from examples. Suppose, for instance, that over the years Anna-Louise has used interpretive counterparts of Jane's beliefs about yoga to build up evidential support for the following generalization:

(22) All of Jane's beliefs about yoga are true.

Suppose also that she has recently decided that she should attribute a new belief about yoga to Jane, and that she uses (23) to attribute this new belief:

(23) Jane believes that I (that is, Anna-Louise) will be more comfortable in difficult yoga postures if I breathe more deeply while I am in them.

Putting (22) and (23) together, Anna-Louise infers (24):

(24) It is true that I will be more comfortable in difficult yoga postures if I breathe more deeply while I am in them.

And this leads in turn to her accepting (25):

(25) I will be more comfortable in difficult yoga postures if I breathe more deeply while I am in them.

Acting on this belief, Anna-Louise soon finds that it is correct. This finding is of course evidence for (22) and (23), but it also argues persuasively for the empirical fruitfulness of the practices that led Anna-Louise to accept (22) in the first place.

It is clear that there is nothing unusual about this case. On the contrary, we encounter cases of the same sort with great frequency in everyday life.

We have found that we have practices that presuppose that interpretive counterparts of inaccessible thoughts are good translations, and also that the practices in question have considerable predictive value. It is easy to see, furthermore, that this predictive success contributes in a variety of ways to our well-being and even to our survival. In view of these facts, it seems appropriate to conclude that we are entirely justified in employing the given practices, and by the same token, in committing ourselves to the proposition about translation that they presuppose.

IX

We have been concerned in the preceding sections with the following two issues:

(P1) If we extend Horwichian minimalism so as to accommodate the phenomenon of indexicality in the simplest and most natural way, we wind up with a definition of truth which contains many clauses that lie beyond the ken of any one agent. But we have intuitions to the effect that it is impossible to possess a concept whose meaning is fixed by a definition unless one fully understands all of the clauses of the definition. Prima facie, at least, these intuitions call the extended Horwichian account of truth into question.

(P2) Our extended Horwichian account of truth implies that the truth condition of a thought is the instance of schema (T) that is concerned with that thought. Accordingly, it can seem that if minimalism is correct, then grasping the truth condition of a thought must consist in understanding and accepting the relevant instance of schema (T). Now it is clearly impossible for an agent to understand and accept instances of (T) that are concerned with thoughts that are inaccessible from the agent's perspective. However, we have strong intuitions to the effect that it is possible for an agent to grasp the truth condition of an indexical thought even if the thought is inaccessible to the agent. So, once again, we find that there appears to be conflict between a consequence of extended Horwichian minimalism and certain of our intuitions.

I have maintained that these problems can be dealt with successfully, and that it is therefore reasonable to think that Horwichian minimalism can be generalized in such a way as to provide a satisfactory account of the truth of indexical propositions.

We must now inquire into the relationship between the problems represented by (P1) and (P2) and the substitutional account of our semantic concepts that is proposed in earlier chapters. Do similar problems arise in connection with the substitutional account? If so, what exactly is the nature of the latter problems? And is it possible to adapt the foregoing solutions to (P1) and (P2) so as to yield solutions to these problems?

When one first considers the matter, it can seem that (P1) has no counterpart among the problems that confront substitutional theories. (P1) arises because Horwichian minimalism proposes an *implicit* definition of truth that has *many* independent clauses. On the other hand, substitutionalism claims that the concept of truth is adequately captured by (S):

(S) For any $x$, $x$ is true if and only if $(\Sigma p)((x = \text{the thought that } p) \text{ and } p)$.

(S) is an *explicit* definition that has *exactly one* clause.

On further reflection, however, it becomes clear that there is a counterpart of problem (P1), after all. To appreciate this, recall that substitutionalism explains the meanings of substitutional quantifiers in terms of the inference patterns that determine the roles of such quantifiers in our reasoning. I will not attempt here to give an exhaustive account of these patterns. It is enough for our present purposes to observe that it is enormously plausible that one of the patterns governing existential substitutional quantification is Existential Introduction:

*Existential Introduction*

$$\frac{(\ldots T \ldots)}{(\Sigma \mathbf{p})(\ldots \mathbf{p} \ldots)} \qquad \frac{(\ldots \mathbf{q} \ldots)}{(\Sigma \mathbf{p})(\ldots \mathbf{p} \ldots)}$$

Here $T$ is a particular, determinate thought, and $(\ldots T \ldots)$ is the particular, determinate thought that comes from replacing all free occurrences of the propositional variable $\mathbf{p}$ in the open thought $(\ldots \mathbf{p} \ldots)$ with $T$. Further, $\mathbf{q}$ is a propositional variable, and $(\ldots \mathbf{q} \ldots)$ is the open thought that comes from replacing all free occurrences of the propositional variable $\mathbf{p}$ in the open thought $(\ldots \mathbf{p} \ldots)$ with free occurrences of $\mathbf{q}$.

Now if it is true, as I am claiming, that Existential Introduction is partially constitutive of the concept of existential substitutional quantification, then it must be the case that the possession condition for that concept requires agents to conform to Existential Introduction. It follows that the possession condition must imply the following proposition: where $x$ is any agent, if $x$ possesses the concept of existential substitutional quantification (hereafter known as the *existential concept*), then $x$ is disposed to infer a thought of the form $(\Sigma \mathbf{p})(\ldots \mathbf{p} \ldots)$ from any thought of the form $(\ldots T \ldots)$. It is here that a difficulty appears to arise. Thus, it can easily appear that this proposition commits us to a further proposition that can be formulated as follows: where $x$ is any agent, if $x$ possesses the existential concept, then $x$ must be capable, at least in principle, of entertaining any thought of the form $(\ldots T \ldots)$. (For how is it possible to have a disposition to infer a conclusion of the form $C$ from a premise of the form $P$ unless one is capable of entertaining both $C$ and $P$?) We know, however, that for any agent $x$, there is an enormous range of thoughts of the given form that $x$ is incapable of entertaining – specifically, the range of indexical thoughts of that form that are inaccessible from $x$'s perspective. It appears to follow that no agent can fulfill the possession condition for the existential concept, and to follow from this in turn that it is a mistake to attempt to analyze truth in terms of substitutional quantification.

In other words, just as Horwichian minimalism appears to come to grief as a result of the fact that there are inaccessible instances of schema (T), so also substitutionalism appears to come to grief as a result of the fact that there are inaccessible instances of Existential Introduction. In the first case, the existence of inaccessible instances appears to show that no agent can possess a Horwichian concept of truth. And in the second case, the existence of inaccessible instances appears to show *both* that no agent can possess the existential concept *and* that no agent can possess a substitutional concept of truth.

Fortunately, our solution to the first problem can easily be adapted so as to yield a solution to the second problem. The first problem is solved by observing that a possession condition for the Horwichian concept of truth need not require that one be disposed to accept every instance of schema (T), but only that one be disposed to accept all of the instances of (T) that one is capable of accepting (provided that it is the formal properties of such instances that elicit one's acceptance). A similar observation holds in the case of the existential concept. In order to possess this concept, it is enough that one be disposed to conform to Existential Introduction in all those cases in which one is capable of understanding the constituent thoughts (provided that it is the formal properties of such instances that are causally responsible for one's conformity). Just as an agent who satisfies the former condition can be said to stand in cognitive relationships to all instances of (T), albeit only mediated relationships in the case of inaccessible thoughts, so also an agent who satisfies the second condition can be said to stand in appropriate cognitive relationships to all instances of Existential Introduction.

It appears, then, that there is no obstacle to saying that ordinary agents are capable of conforming to Existential Introduction, nor to saying that they are capable of conforming to whatever other inference patterns figure in the possession condition for the existential concept. That is, it is possible to say such things even while also maintaining that Existential Introduction and other such inference patterns have instances that involve inaccessible thoughts. It follows that any theory of truth that is based on (S) can appropriately be regarded as explaining our thought and talk about the truth of indexical thoughts, including even those parts of that thought and talk that involve intercontextual propositions. This is true, in particular, of extended substitutionalism, the theory of truth that is presented in Chapters 2 and 3.

Let us turn now to consider what would happen if we were to attempt to supplement extended substitutionalism with an account of what is involved in grasping the truth condition of an inaccessible thought. Would we encounter a counterpart of problem (P2) above?

Yes. Extended substitutionalism should be understood as making a claim about truth conditions that coincides with the claim that is made by Horwichian minimalism – specifically, that the truth condition of a thought is the instance of schema (T) that is concerned with that thought. (I remind the reader that substitutionalism is no less respectful than minimalism of the intuition that the concept of truth is constitutively linked with instances of (T). As we saw in the first appendix to Chapter 2, definition (S) implies all propositions of form (T).) It follows immediately that substitutionalism confronts a problem that is a counterpart of (P2) above. Indeed, it confronts a problem that is identical with (P2). Thus, it must explain what is involved in grasping a truth condition in such a way as to accommodate the fact that agents are logically precluded from entertaining instances of (T) that are concerned with inaccessible thoughts. As we saw in Section VI of the present chapter, it can seem that the task of giving such an explanation is not an easy one.

Fortunately, we know from Sections VII and VIII that it is in the end possible to construct a satisfactory explanation of grasping. It suffices to distinguish between direct and indirect grasping, and to add definitions (G**), (IG), and (TR) to extended substitutionalism. It is clear that extended substitutionalism has every bit as much right as minimalism to avail itself of this solution.

I conclude this chapter by noting that extended substitutionalism also employs a second conception of truth conditions. On this second conception, the truth condition of a thought is the state of affairs that is connected with the thought by the relation of semantic correspondence. Thus, for instance, on this second conception, the truth condition of the thought that snow is white is the state of affairs *snow's being white*. Now it is tempting to say that one grasps a truth condition of this second type by understanding and accepting a thought of the following form:

The thought that *p* is true if and only if the state of affairs that *p* is actual.

But if one yields to the temptation to say this, then of course one faces a problem that closely parallels problem (P2). Fortunately, reflection shows that this parallel problem admits of a solution that parallels the solution to problem (P2). It suffices to distinguish between direct and indirect grasping, and to adopt definitions that are similar to (G★★), (IG), and (TR).


APPENDIX

The contemporary literature on *linguistic* indexicality suggests a way of approaching questions about the semantic properties of indexical thoughts that is quite different from the approach I have taken in the present chapter. Although this alternative approach has not been widely discussed in print, there is reason to think that it has achieved a certain degree of conversational currency. Accordingly, it may be helpful to say a few words about it here.

Among philosophers of language, there appears to be wide interest in developing an idea about the semantic concepts we use in connection with indexical *sentences* that Davidson made famous in "Truth and Meaning."[10] That is to say, there appears to be wide interest in the project of explaining our talk of the truth and falsity of indexical sentences in terms of a truth predicate that is defined in Tarskian or quasi-Tarskian fashion, but that differs from standard Tarskian truth predicates in that it is relativized to such features of contexts as speakers and times.

As the reader may recall, Davidson urged in "Truth and Meaning" that it may be possible to explain our thought and talk about the truth of indexical sentences in terms of propositions like (★):

(★) "I am tired" is true as (potentially) spoken by *p* at *t* if and only if *p* is tired at *t*.

Here, of course, we have a concept of truth that has three argument places, one for sentence *types*, one for speakers, and one for times. Davidson claimed that it might be possible to explain this relativized notion in

Tarskian fashion, that is, by defining it explicitly in terms of a notion of satisfaction. The notion of satisfaction that figured in the definition would have to be different from the standard Tarskian notion, because it would have to be appropriately relativized to speakers and times. But still, Davidson maintained, there would be enough similarity that it would be appropriate to see the resulting construction as an extension of Tarski's work to the indexical domain.

(Satisfaction is a relation that links sequences of objects from a universe of discourse to sentence types. I must here presuppose an understanding of this relation, referring the reader who is not familiar with it to the excellent introductory accounts that are available in the literature.[11])

Now, it might be thought that it would be a good idea to approach questions about the semantic concepts we use in connection with indexical *thoughts* in a similar way. Thus, it might be thought to be both possible and desirable to see those concepts as applying in the first instance to determinable representations rather than determinate representations, and as having argument places for various features of contexts. More concretely, it might be thought possible and desirable to define such a relativistic concept of truth in terms of a relativistic concept of satisfaction, more or less in Tarski's way, and to then derive truth conditions for individual thoughts. These truth conditions would be counterparts of ($\star$). Thus, they would look like ($\star\star$):

($\star\star$) The (determinable) thought that I am tired is true as entertained by $p$ at $t$ if and only if $p$ is tired at $t$.

Finally, it might be held that the concept of truth that we use in connection with determinate indexical thoughts could somehow be defined reductively in terms of the relativistic concept that figures in ($\star\star$).

Here, then, is an alternative to the approach that is recommended above. I have several reasons for preferring the latter approach, but I will just mention the one that admits of the most compact formulation.

My goal is to explain semantic concepts in a way that reflects the actual structure of our conceptual scheme. It is at least prima facie plausible that AHM and SEM succeed in capturing definitional relations that actually exist. On the other hand, it seems highly implausible, both prima facie and secunda facie, that our ordinary concept of truth is governed by a Tarskian definition.

Any claim to the effect that our ordinary concept of truth admits of a Tarskian characterization is rendered problematic by the fact that a concept of truth cannot count as Tarskian unless it is explicitly defined in terms of a concept of satisfaction. It is quite clear that human thinkers are incapable of defining the concept of truth that they apply to thoughts in terms of satisfaction, for it is quite clear that they lack a concept of satisfaction that can be used in connection with the realm of thoughts. (Consider the sequence $\langle 1, 2, 3, \ldots \rangle$. Does it satisfy the thought that all positive integers are even or odd? I do not know what this question means – unless, of course, I take it to have a kind of borrowed meaning, a meaning that derives from its formal similarity to certain questions that are concerned with sentences in artificial languages.)

The concept of satisfaction is a technical concept that owes its meaning to formal definitions that place severe restrictions on its scope. That is to say, its meaning is entirely immanent to discussions of artificial languages – more specifically, to discussions of the language of first order logic and certain extensions thereof. These languages have very little in common, either formally or semantically, with the realm of thoughts.

It is clear, then, that satisfaction is not a commonsense concept. It follows that it could not possibly play a role in fixing the meaning of the commonsense notion of truth.

# 5

## *Why Meaning Matters*

I

The present chapter is concerned with questions about the practical and theoretical utility of semantic concepts.

Questions that are concerned with the utility of *truth* have received a great deal of attention in the literature, and there are several well developed explanations of its utility in the field. We took note of one of these explanations in Chapter 2, when we considered W. V. Quine's suggestion that truth is useful primarily because it provides us with the ability to make indefinite and generalized endorsements. According to Quine, if we find truth indispensable, this is because it enables us to affirm thoughts that we are unwilling or unable to formulate explicitly, as when we express agreement with Fermat's Last Theorem by thinking that the Theorem is now widely accepted, and is therefore probably true, and because it enables us to affirm simultaneously all of the members of large (and possibly infinite) collections of thoughts, as when we affirm that all of the propositions that follow from General Relativity have turned out to be more or less true.

Now as I see it, Quine has identified the main functions of the concept of truth: other authors have identified additional functions, but these additional functions can generally be seen to presuppose, in one way or another, the Quinean functions.[1] Accordingly, I propose here to set questions about the utility of truth aside, and to focus on questions about the utility of our relational semantic concepts – that is, of reference, denotation, semantic correspondence, and their fellows. Comparatively little has been said about this second group of questions. In fact, while it is generally acknowledged that the family of relational semantic concepts is important to us, the nature of that importance remains shrouded in mystery. This is

89

particularly true of the notion of semantic correspondence. I will attempt in this chapter to lay the foundations of a more balanced understanding of our semantic concerns and commitments.

I will maintain that the utility of relational semantic concepts derives primarily from the following two facts: They provide the basis for generating a system of categories that can be used in classifying thoughts and propositional attitudes, and they make it possible for us to frame generalizations that describe relationships between conceptually informed representations and constituents of extraconceptual reality.

I will illustrate the first fact by describing the way in which the notion of *aboutness* contributes to the formation of new classificatory concepts. Using this notion, we can, for example, form the concept of beliefs about Nixon, the concept of beliefs about Carter, the concept of beliefs about Reagan, and the concept of beliefs about Bush. Further, we can form the concept of Carter's beliefs about Nixon, the concept of Reagan's beliefs about Nixon, and the concept of Bush's beliefs about Nixon. Still further, we can form the concept of Carter's perceptually grounded beliefs about Nixon, the concept of Carter's testimonially grounded beliefs about Nixon, and the concept of Carter's inductively grounded beliefs about Nixon. And so on. Evidently, the concept of aboutness provides the basis for a taxonomic system that is extremely powerful – a taxonomic system that makes an infinite number of distinctions. Moreover, the classifications that this system enables are often extremely useful, making it possible, for example, for us to formulate claims about the reliability of various agents and various sources of information of other kinds.

The discussion of aboutness is confined to Section II. In Sections III–V, I discuss the second source of the utility of relational semantic concepts, the fact that they make it possible for us to formulate generalizations that describe connections between the conceptual order and extraconceptual reality. To illustrate this fact, I cite a number of generalizations from folk psychology. Some of these generalizations are a priori, while others are a posteriori, being known on the basis of their ability to explain the behaviors that we witness in our fellow creatures. My coverage of these generalizations will be fairly extensive, for I am concerned not only to establish that relational semantic concepts are useful (a claim that could be sustained, after all, by showing only that they are not completely lacking in utility), but to make a case for the view that such concepts make an important contribution to knowledge, a contribution that is both indispensable and very broad in scope.

I have a second reason for dwelling at length on the role that relational concepts play in folk psychology. In recent years philosophers have shown considerable interest in questions about the relationships between semantic concepts and such "material" or "naturalistic" notions as causation, information, and reliable indication. I believe that we can see the answers to these questions, or at least substantial portions of the answers, by considering the role that relational concepts play in folk psychological generalizations. The answers that emerge are less dramatic than the ones that have sometimes been anticipated. Thus, they have no tendency to suggest that semantic notions are coextensive with "naturalistic" notions, and therefore no tendency to suggest that semantic facts are reducible to natural facts. But they do indicate that there are broad, systematic connections between the semantic realm and the realm of natural fact.

The themes of earlier chapters will not figure explicitly in the present one. In particular, there will be no explicit discussion of the pros and cons of substitutionalism. At a deeper level, however, it is true that we will be concerned with substitutionalism on every page. If there are features of our relational semantic concepts that are incompatible with substitutionalism, those features would presumably come to the fore at some point in an investigation of the practical and theoretical utility of the concepts. No such features will be brought to light by our inquiries here. Thus, at the end of the day, we will be able to claim that substitutionalism has survived an important test. I allow myself to hope that this will bring the reader a step closer to full acceptance of substitutionalism.

II

It is useful and even essential in life to have on hand a stock of correct generalizations about the reliability of one's own cognitive faculties, and also a stock of correct generalizations about the reliability of various external sources of propositional information (such as other agents, news agencies, brokerage houses, and so on). Thus, for example, it can be quite useful to know that the following generalizations are correct:

(1) When an agent's visual faculties are functioning properly, and the agent is viewing an object under standard conditions of illumination, etc., the agent's visual beliefs are quite likely to be true.
(2) When they are speaking *ex officio*, representatives of the Congressional Budget Office tend to be highly reliable.

In framing such generalizations, one is always involved, in one way or another, with the concept of truth. This is because the relevant notion of reliability is definable in terms of truth: to say that a source of propositional information is reliable is to say that its deliverances are quite likely to be true. Thus, if a reliability principle does not make explicit use of the notion of truth, it will be implicitly concerned with truth, either because it deploys the notion of reliability itself, or because it deploys some cognate notion, such as the notion of trustworthiness.

There are of course a great many significant reliability principles that closely resemble (1) and (2). It appears, however, that there is an even larger number of reliability principles which have a feature that our two examples lack. Specifically, it appears that most such principles contain some sort of device that restricts their scope to thoughts or propositional attitudes that are concerned with a particular subject matter. There are various devices that we use to restrict reliability principles in this way, but there can be no doubt that the concept of aboutness is the one that we rely on most frequently. Thus, every human agent maintains an extensive data base consisting of principles like the following:

(3) I have learned over the years that my intuitions about my daughter's moods are reasonably reliable.
(4) Warren Goldfarb's opinions about the decision problem are always correct.
(5) *The Times* is an extremely reliable source of information about New York restaurants.

As (3)–(5) attest, the notion of aboutness plays an absolutely crucial role in our practice of forming and using reliability principles. Most of the time, qualifications having to do with aboutness are essential to the truth of reliability principles. (It would be a mistake to project reliability over the whole range of my intuitions. Also, while it is no doubt true that Warren Goldfarb's opinions about matters other than the decision problem tend on the whole to be sound, he would be the first to agree, I feel sure, that he occasionally lapses into error. Etc.)

The utility of aboutness is due to its ability to support a system of categories that we can use in classifying thoughts and propositional attitudes. These categories can be large or small, homogeneous or variegated, familiar or *recherché*, straightforward or Byzantine (as in the case of the category determined by the concept *view held by Nixon about Dean's pronouncements about Nixon's own initial description of the situation*). By including this one notion in our conceptual scheme, we gain access to a potentially infinite set of categories that would otherwise be closed off to us.

In view of these considerations, it is clear that the notion of aboutness is extremely useful. But we are supposed to be considering the utility of relational semantic concepts. Does the notion of aboutness count as semantic? Well, it is easy to see that the content of the notion can at least be *partially* characterized in semantic terms, for it is easy to see that there are conceptually true propositions that link the notion to semantic notions. Here are two examples:

(A1) Where $T$ is any thought, $C$ is any singular concept, and $x$ is any object, if it is the case (a) that $C$ is a constituent of $T$ and (b) that $C$ refers to $x$, then $T$ is about $x$.

(A2) Where $T$ is any thought, $C$ is any quantificational concept that counts as universal, and $x$ is any object, if it is the case (a) that $C$ is a constituent of $T$ and (b) that $x$ falls within the range of $C$, then $T$ is about $x$.

Two explanatory comments: First, "constituent" here means "constituent that does not occur within the scope of an intensional concept of some sort." And second, where $C$ is a quantificational concept that counts as universal and $x$ is any object, $x$ is said to fall within the range of $C$ if and only if either (a) $C$ is a pure universal quantifier (e.g., *everything*) or (b) $C$ is a complex concept consisting of a universal quantifier and a general concept $G$ (e.g., $C$ has the form *every G*) and $G$ denotes $x$.

That (A1) and (A2) are conceptually true can be seen by considering examples. First, with reference to (A1), observe that it is conceptually true that if the concept of Socrates refers to the teacher of Plato, then the thought that Socrates is wise is about the teacher of Plato. And second, with reference to (A2), observe that if the concept of a philosopher denotes Socrates, then the thought that every philosopher is wise is about Socrates.

It follows from (A1) and (A2) that claims of aboutness sometimes owe their truth to facts involving the relations of reference and denotation. Whether or not the notion of aboutness counts fully as a semantic concept, it is possible to use the notion to give expression to semantic facts.

I will not attempt here to assess the claim that the concept of aboutness is entirely semantic in character, for that would be an enormously complex undertaking. Thus, to mention only one of the issues that would have to be addressed, it seems entirely possible that the expression "*the* concept of aboutness" is misleading – that there are two or more concepts that deserve the label "concept of aboutness." Even the task of settling this preliminary issue would be difficult.[2]

Fortunately, for our present purposes, it suffices that the following four propositions be correct: First, that the concept of aboutness is extremely useful; second, that the utility of this concept can be explained, at least in part, by adverting to its role in generating a system of concepts for classifying thoughts and propositional attitudes; third, that the content of the concept is at least partly semantic; and fourth, that the usefulness of the concept is at least partially owing to the semantic portion of its content. Perhaps enough has been said already to establish that these propositions deserve our esteem.

III

In addition to enabling useful classifications of thoughts and attitudes, relational concepts are valuable because they make it possible for us to formulate generalizations that describe relationships between conceptually informed representations and constituents of extraconceptual reality. I wish to turn now to consider this second source of utility. I will illustrate it by taking a fairly close look at the role that relational concepts play in folk psychology. My hope is to convey a sense of the scope of this role and also a sense of its indispensability.

The role in question has two dimensions – one that is a priori and one that is a posteriori. Now it turns out that the a priori dimension is largely bound up with questions about the *possession conditions* of concepts – that is, with questions about the conditions under which particular concepts can be said to be possessed by particular agents. Accordingly, it will be to our advantage to begin this part of our discussion by taking a look at the nature of possession conditions. I believe that the best way to do this is to review a couple of the claims about possession conditions that are put forward in Christopher Peacocke's *A Study of Concepts*.[3]

The first of these claims is the doctrine that concepts are always *individuated* by possession conditions. In other words, Peacocke maintains that for every concept $C$, there is a set of conditions that are individually necessary and jointly sufficient for possession of $C$, and that by formulating these conditions one can fully specify the essential nature of $C$.

The second claim is the doctrine that the question of whether an agent possesses a given concept $C$ will always depend on considerations having to do with the agent's actual and potential propositional attitudes toward thoughts in which $C$ figures as a constituent (hereafter $C$-*thoughts*). To be more specific, Peacocke maintains that possession of $C$ will always depend on factors of one or more of the following five kinds: the agent's actual propositional attitudes toward $C$-thoughts; the agent's dispositions to form new attitudes toward $C$-thoughts by inference from other attitudes; the agent's dispositions to form new attitudes toward $C$-thoughts by inference from experiential encounters with reality; the agent's dispositions to pass inferentially from attitudes toward $C$-thoughts to other attitudes; and the agent's dispositions to pass from attitudes toward $C$-thoughts to states of readiness for action.

What exactly do possession conditions that invoke such factors look like? This question is best answered by quoting some of the examples that Peacocke provides. One such example is the following possession condition for the concept of conjunction:[4]

Conjunction is that concept $C$ to possess which a thinker must find transitions that are of the following forms primitively compelling, and must do so because they are of these forms:

$$\frac{\begin{array}{c} p \\ q \end{array}}{pCq} \qquad \frac{pCq}{p} \qquad \frac{pCq}{q}$$

Peacocke is not altogether explicit about the intended sense of "primitively compelling," but it is not too hard to see roughly what he has in mind. Thus, it is clear that if an agent can be said to find certain arguments involving a concept primitively compelling, in Peacocke's sense of the expression "primitively compelling," then the agent must be disposed to pass from premises of arguments of the given forms to the appropriate conclusions, and to do so in a manner that is characterized by confidence and a sense of appropriateness. Moreover, this disposition must be basic in the sense that it does not derive from other inferential dispositions involving the same concept.

Peacocke's possession condition for the concept *red* provides us with another fairly straightforward example. It runs as follows:

The concept *red* is that concept $C$ to possess which a thinker must meet these conditions:

1. He must be disposed to believe a content that consists of a singular perceptual-demonstrative mode of presentation $m$ in predicational combination with $C$ when the perceptual experience that makes $m$ available presents its object in a red' region of the object's visual field and does so in conditions he takes to be normal, and when in addition he takes his perceptual mechanisms to be working properly. The thinker must also be disposed to form the belief for the reason that the object is so presented.

2. The thinker must be disposed to believe a content consisting of any singular mode of predication $k$ not meeting all the conditions on $m$ in (1) when he takes its object to have the primary quality ground (if any) of the disposition of objects to cause experiences of the sort mentioned in (1).[5]

Roughly speaking, part 1 of this proposal represents possession of the concept *red* as depending on a disposition to make certain sorts of perceptual judgment in response to sensory information that attests to the presence of red objects in the visual environment. (The primed expression "red'" stands for the property of being phenomenally red, that is, for the sensational property that is exemplified by part of the visual field of a normal subject when he or she is viewing a red object under normal conditions of observation.) Part 2 is intended, among other things, to accommodate the fact that an agent who possesses the concept of red must be disposed to arrive at certain beliefs involving the concept as a result of inference from other beliefs. Although it is unlikely that either of these conditions is entirely correct as it stands, the proposal does enjoy a considerable amount of intuitive appeal.

To summarize: I will be borrowing the following two claims from Peacocke: first, the claim that concepts are individuated by their possession conditions; and second, the claim that questions of possession always depend on questions about an agent's actual and potential propositional attitudes.

In addition to these two Peacockean assumptions, I will here assume that possession conditions often depend in part on "material" or "natural" relations (e.g., causal and informational relations) that link the cognitive states and processes involving a concept to extramental objects and properties. It is part of this assumption that, for example, the answer to the question of whether an agent possesses the concept of water depends in part on whether the agent possesses a concept whose use has historically been shaped, in part at least, by information that derives directly or indirectly from actual samples of water. In making this third assumption, I am not really departing from the spirit of Peacocke's theory; it is clear that some such idea is implicit in his work. (Cf. the earlier discussion of the possession condition for the concept *red*.) It appears, however, that the assumption is sufficiently important to warrant explicit mention. (The assumption is fully compatible with Peacocke's doctrine that possession always depends on facts involving actual and potential propositional attitudes, for it claims only that in many cases possession depends *in part* on material or natural connections with extramental entities.)

IV

We have been reviewing Peacocke's theory of possession conditions with a view to obtaining a suitable foundation for a discussion of the role that relational semantic concepts play in generalizations that articulate the a priori portion of folk psychology. We can now turn to the task of formulating some generalizations of this sort. I will begin by citing some examples that make use of the concept of semantic expression (i.e., the concept that figures in the claim that the notion *red* expresses the property *being red*).

As we observed in Chapter 2, in the 1970s, Kripke and Putnam cited a number of examples and thought experiments which provide support for the view that possession of natural kind concepts depends on having interacted causally with instances of the properties that the concepts express. It appears that the following principle is one of the implications of their work:

(7) Let $C$ be a natural kind concept that semantically expresses the property $\phi$, and let it be the case that $\phi$ is a natural kind that is observationally accessible. Given these assumptions, if $x$ is an agent who possesses $C$ at time $T$, then it must be the case that $x$ satisfies the following condition: it has been true at times prior to $T$, generally speaking, that when $x$ has been led by normal perceptual processes to make a recognitional judgment involving $C$, one of the distal causes of $x$'s judgment has been an instance of the property $\phi$.

It appears that (7) is true, and also that we can know it to be true a priori.

(An aside: (7) is intended as an idealization. Thus, as it is formulated here, (7) fails to allow for the fact that possession of natural kind concepts can be grounded in dispositions to defer to other members of one's linguistic community rather than causal relations to samples of the relevant kinds. In other words, it fails to allow for the fact that possession can be grounded in dispositions to accept the classificatory judgments of other agents whom one takes to be more knowledgeable than oneself. While it is important to take such complexities into account in other contexts, they do not affect the points at issue here. I will continue to idealize away from them in the way that is represented by (7). Further, (7) fails to allow for the fact that in some cases possession of kind concepts is not grounded in causal/recognitional relations between users of the concepts and instances of kinds, but rather in reference-fixing stipulations (i.e., in stipulations to the effect that concepts shall have the same reference as descriptions that are independently known to pick out kinds). As with the first idealization, this second idealization will continue to be in effect in the sequel.)

Now in order to possess a kind concept, it would seem that it is not enough to have a history of interacting causally with items to which the concept applies. One must also be disposed to continue one's practice of applying the concept to such items. Thus, it appears to be true, and to be knowable a priori, that possession of kind concepts obeys the following additional principle:

(8) Let $C$ be a natural kind concept that expresses the property $\phi$, and let $\phi$ be a natural kind that is observationally accessible. Given these assumptions, if $x$ is an agent who possesses $C$, then it must be the case that $x$ satisfies the following condition: on occasions when (a) $x$'s perceptual apparatus is functioning properly, (b) $x$'s sense experience is such as to make it likely that an instance of $\phi$ is in $x$'s vicinity, and (c) $x$ entertains the question *is there a (sample of) C nearby?*, then, provided that $x$ is not in possession of a belief that calls the available sensory evidence into question, $x$ will come to believe the proposition *there is a (sample of) C nearby*.[6]

Like (7), (8) can be seen to hold by considering various possible agents in relation to particular natural kind concepts, in each case weighing the question of whether it seems appropriate to ascribe the relevant kind concept to the relevant agent. The notion of semantic expression enters the picture when one attempts to capture one's intuitions about particular cases by general principles. In order to state such principles, it is necessary either to appeal to a semantic relation or to avail oneself of the apparatus of substitutional quantification.

(7) and (8) are concerned only with observational concepts that express natural kinds, but there are counterparts of (7) and (8) that have a much broader range. Indeed, it seems that there are very general variants of (7) and (8) that apply to the whole range of observational concepts – to observational kind concepts, to be sure, but also to observational concepts that express purely perceptual properties, such as colors, shapes, sizes, and forms of motion.

In addition to these more general principles, there are also principles involving the notion of expression that have a more restricted range. Thus, for example, there is a principle that applies specifically to those observational kind concepts that qualify as *sortals*. Roughly speaking, a sortal concept is a concept that is associated with principles that determine the spatiotemporal boundaries of the objects to which the concept applies. Thus, for example, the concept *rabbit* is a sortal concept because anyone who counts as possessing it is able to make individuative judgments that correspond to the spatiotemporal boundaries of individual rabbits – to judge, for example, that a certain line constitutes the boundary between a female rabbit and her nursing offspring. Now many observational kind concepts are also sortal concepts – *rabbit* is an example, and so are *grain of sand*, *raindrop*, *tree*, and *finger*. Like all observational kind concepts, observational kind concepts that are sortals satisfy (7) and (8). But they also satisfy an additional principle that runs as follows:

(9) Let $C$ be a sortal kind concept that expresses a property $\phi$, and let $\phi$ be a sortal kind that is observationally accessible. Under these assumptions, if $x$ is an agent who possesses $C$, then it must be the case that $x$ satisfies the following condition: $x$ is disposed to use $C$ in observationally grounded individuative judgments that reflect the spatiotemporal boundaries of instances of $\phi$.

There are a number of ways in which judgments can reflect the spatiotemporal boundaries of objects, but it will suffice for our purposes to mention a couple. So, in the first place: Suppose that an agent is disposed to accept thoughts of the form *this rabbit is white* when and only when he or she is confronted with a rabbit whose surface is entirely white (so that, for example, the agent will not accept a thought of the given form when an otherwise black rabbit has a white spot on its side). Such an agent is disposed to make judgments that reflect the spatial boundaries of rabbits.[7] Second: Suppose that an agent is disposed to accept thoughts of the form *this rabbit is identical with that rabbit* when and only these conditions are satisfied: (a) his or her use of the demonstrative concept *this rabbit* is temporarily controlled by perceptual information about a certain rabbit $r_1$; (b) his or her use of the demonstrative concept *that rabbit* is temporarily controlled by perceptual information about a certain rabbit $r_2$; and (c) $r_1$ is identical with $r_2$. Such is an agent whose judgments reflect the spatial boundaries of rabbits and also their temporal boundaries.[8,9]

In addition to generalizations that are concerned exclusively with kind concepts, there are others that are concerned with concepts of quite different sorts. Thus, in the first place, Kripke's work suggests that there is a variant of (7) that applies to an enormous range of concepts that stand for individual substances. To be more specific, Kripke's work suggests that something like the following is true: If an agent possesses a nominal concept that refers to a spatiotemporal particular, then it must be the case that the agent's acquisition of the concept was shaped by causal traces of the particular – for example, by utterances of other agents that were themselves due, ultimately, to states of affairs involving the particular. (As in the case of (7), I am simplifying here by prescinding from cases in which agents possess concepts in virtue of having fixed their reference with descriptions that are known on independent grounds to refer.) Furthermore, it appears that there are variants of (7) and (8) which apply to general concepts that express *theoretical* natural kinds – that is, to concepts such as *hydrogen atom* and *black hole*. Of course, principles that are concerned with concepts that express theoretical kinds could not speak of direct perceptual interactions between agents and samples of kinds. Rather, they will be concerned with perceptual interactions between agents and experimental traces of samples of kinds. Apart from this difference, however, the relevant principles will be quite similar to (7) and (8). Finally, it is plausible that there is a variant of (9) that applies to theoretical sortal concepts.

It appears, then, that the family of principles that includes (7), (8), and (9) is quite large, and that it has implications concerning all concepts that stand for spatiotemporal entities. But this is not the end of the story. There are also principles which apply to concepts that designate various sorts of abstract entity. I will illustrate this with an example involving an important class of arithmetical concepts. To appreciate the example, observe that arithmetical concepts appear to fall into three categories: There are concepts that we possess in virtue of having accepted explicit definitions, concepts that we possess in virtue of having accepted implicit definitions, and concepts that we possess in virtue of having mastered computational procedures. My example is concerned with concepts that belong to the third category – specifically, with concepts that count as *computational*. It can be formulated as follows:

(10) Let $C$ be a computational arithmetical concept that stands for a dyadic arithmetical function $\mathbf{f}$. Given this assumption, if $x$ possesses $C$, then it must be the case that $x$ possesses a computational procedure $P$ involving $C$ such that $P$ satisfies the following condition: If $P$ were realized in an "ideal agent" (i.e., an agent with unlimited working memory and computation time), and the agent applied $P$ to the numerical concepts $m$ and $n$, then $P$ would cause the agent to believe the thought $mCn = p$ if and only if, where $w$, $y$ and $z$ are the natural numbers that serve as the referents of $m$, $n$, and $p$, respectively, $z$ is the number that results when the function $\mathbf{f}$ is applied to $w$ and $y$.

In effect, (10) tells us that if $x$ possesses a computational concept that stands for a dyadic arithmetical function, then $x$ must possess a computational procedure which, if realized in an ideal agent, would lead that agent to make elementary numerical judgments involving that concept in such a way as to mirror the elementary facts in which that function is involved. Or, to adapt a piece of jargon from metamathematics, $x$'s use of the concept must be governed by a computational procedure that would enable the (potential) beliefs of an ideal agent to "numeralwise represent" the function.

It appears, then, that notions like semantic expression, reference, and standing for make it possible for us to frame general principles concerning possession conditions – principles that articulate the ways in which possession of concepts depends on such factors as causation, perception, individuative correspondence, and numeralwise representation. We have found that this class of principles is large and heterogeneous. Moreover, reflection shows that it would be easy to expand our little sample to include principles that attested to an even greater degree of heterogeneity. Thus, for example, it shows that there are a priori semantic principles that generalize across the range of possession conditions for psychological concepts.

It might be asked here whether it is legitimate to describe the knowledge expressed by principles like (7)–(10) as important knowledge. After all, (7)–(10) appear to have little direct relevance to such basic folk psychological goals as predicting and explaining behavior. Moreover, unlike the principles we will consider in the next section, (7)–(10) have little direct relevance to such endeavors as explaining why the mind succeeds in achieving its ends. I think we can see, however, that without principles like (7)–(10), we would have no general knowledge of what concepts *are*, and that this fact lends them considerable theoretical importance. As we observed, it is one of Peacocke's main contentions that concepts are *individuated* by their possession conditions. This view is surely correct. And by the same token, it is correct to say that principles like (7)–(10) add significantly to our understanding of the identity conditions of concepts. It follows that principles like (7)–(10) will inevitably be foundational with respect to any attempt to develop a systematic account of the nature of concepts.

V

In addition to these a priori principles about semantic relations, folk psychology also contains a number of principles about semantic relations that qualify as a posteriori. I turn now to generalizations of this second sort.

Our primary business in this section will be with the notion of semantic correspondence. But it is worth noticing that there is also an important family of a posteriori folk principles that are concerned with the concept of semantic expression. To appreciate the nature of this family, we need to freshen our memory of (7) from the previous section:

(7) Let $C$ be a natural kind concept that semantically expresses the property $\phi$, and let it be the case that $\phi$ is a natural kind that is observationally accessible. Given these assumptions, if $x$ is an agent who possesses $C$ at time $T$, then it must be the case that $x$ satisfies the following condition: it has been true at times prior to $T$, generally speaking, that when $x$ has been led by normal perceptual processes to make a recognitional judgment involving $C$, one of the distal causes of $x$'s judgment has been an instance of the property $\phi$.

(7) tells us that in order to qualify as possessing a kind concept $C$, $x$ must have had a certain sort of history – specifically, a history of responding conceptually to causal signals, transduced perceptually, from instances of the property that $C$ expresses. Now in normal cases, if $x$ qualifies as possessing $C$ in virtue of having had a history of the sort described in (7), then, as a matter of empirical fact, $x$ will continue to respond conceptually in the relevant ways to causal signals emanating from instances of the given property. That is to say, in a normal case, in addition to satisfying (7), an agent will also satisfy the following claim:

(11) Let $C$ be a natural kind concept that semantically expresses the property $\phi$, and let it be the case that $\phi$ is a natural kind that is observationally accessible. Given these assumptions, if $x$ is an agent who possesses $C$, then it is generally the case that when $x$ is led by a normal perceptual process to make a recognitional judgment involving $C$, one of the distal causes of $x$'s judgment is an instance of $\phi$.

Unlike (7), (11) is neither a priori nor necessary. Thus, we can easily imagine situations in which it fails to hold. (Consider, for example, a situation in which an agent with a normal history comes under the control of an evil neuroscientist – a neuroscientist who artificially stimulates the agent's brain in such a way as to cause a steady stream of delusive perceptual experiences.) Instead of being the product of a priori reflection, our knowledge of (11) is due to exposure to the facts of the world.

(11) is just one member of a rather large family. To see that this is so, recall that principle (7) has a number of siblings and cousins that are concerned with concepts other than those that express observationally accessible natural kinds. (Thus, for example, as we noticed, there is a

sibling of (7) that is concerned with concepts that express theoretical natural kinds.) (11) has siblings and cousins that correspond to the siblings and cousins of (7).

Turning now to a posteriori principles about the relation of semantic correspondence, let us begin by taking note of a family of principles whose members are concerned, in effect, with the distal aetiologies of beliefs produced by our "foundational" cognitive faculties – that is, by perception, introspection, and memory. This family includes the following propositions:

(12) Generally speaking, if $x$ is an agent who comes to believe the thought $y$ as a result of perception, and $z$ is the state of affairs that semantically corresponds to $y$, then, provided that $x$'s perceptual mechanisms are functioning properly, $z$ is a distal cause of $x$'s belief.

(13) Generally speaking, if $x$ is an agent who comes to believe the thought $y$ as a result of introspection, and $z$ is the state of affairs that semantically corresponds to $y$, then, provided that $x$'s introspective mechanisms are functioning properly, $z$ is a distal cause of $x$'s belief.

(14) Generally speaking, if $x$ is an agent who comes to believe the thought $y$ as a result of autobiographical memory, and $z$ is the state of affairs that semantically corresponds to $y$, then, provided that $x$'s memorial mechanisms are functioning properly, and provided also that the relevant perceptual and/or introspective mechanisms were functioning properly on the occasion to which $y$ refers, $z$ is a distal cause of $x$'s belief.

As noted, these principles are concerned with aetiological issues: They describe certain aspects of the causal histories of beliefs that are epistemically fundamental. But they can also be thought of as principles of reliable indication. Thus, clearly, it is impossible for a belief to be caused by a state of affairs unless the state of affairs actually obtains. It follows that one of the implications of (12)–(14) is that in normal situations, beliefs formed by perception, introspection, and memory are reliable indicators of how things stand in the realm of extraconceptual fact.

(12)–(14) help to explain why it makes sense for creatures with our interests and ambitions to concern ourselves with semantic correspondence. In addition, they help us to see why it is natural and appropriate for us to prefer an involvement with semantic correspondence to involvements with other thought-world relations that might be imagined. (12)–(14) both deepen and extend our knowledge of the patterns of interaction between mind and world. It is clear that we need a general concept of thought-world correspondence in order to frame principles that carry these benefits. And it is also clear that of the various thought-world relations that might be imagined, there is only a highly restricted subset that could fulfill this condition. (Most concepts of thought-world relations would turn (12)–(14) into falsehoods if we substituted them for the notion of semantic correspondence.) The importance of semantic correspondence is due in part to the fact that it belongs to this highly restrictive subset.

As we observed, (12)–(14) can be thought of both as principles of distal aetiology and as principles of reliable indication. There are other principles about semantic correspondence that have this dual character – for example, principles to the effect that beliefs that are proximally caused by verbal testimony tend to have causal histories that include the states of affairs to which they semantically correspond. But there are also some interesting principles about semantic correspondence that specify patterns of reliable indication but that have little or nothing to say about aetiological questions.

These additional laws of reliability are concerned primarily with the outputs of inferential faculties. Here is one that is concerned with deductive inference:

(15) Generally speaking, if it is the case (a) that $x$ arrives at the thought $w$ from the thoughts $y_1, \ldots, y_n$ by deductive inference, (b) that $y_1, \ldots, y_n$ semantically correspond respectively to the states of affairs $z_1, \ldots, z_n$, and (c) that $w$ semantically corresponds to the state of affairs $u$, then, provided that $x$'s deductive mechanisms are functioning properly, $u$ is logically implied by the set consisting of $z_1, \ldots, z_n$.

(15) tells us, in effect, that deductive inference is generally trustworthy: it tells us that when we move deductively from a given set of thoughts to another one, the state of affairs corresponding to the latter thought will generally obtain if the states of affairs corresponding to the former thoughts obtain. This is, clearly, an important truth, a truth that is well worth knowing. It can contribute to explanations of the representational powers of the mind, and it can also provide support for useful epistemological norms.

There are principles similar to (15) that are concerned with the various forms of inductive inference. Here, for example, is one that is concerned with Baconian enumerative induction:

(16) Generally speaking, if it is the case (a) that $x$ arrives at a thought $w$ of the form *every F is a G* by enumerative inference from a set of thoughts $y_1, \ldots, y_n$,

(b) that the thoughts $y_1, \ldots, y_n$ correspond respectively to the states of affairs $z_1, \ldots, z_n$, and (c) that $w$ corresponds semantically to the state of affairs $u$, then, provided that $x$'s inductive mechanisms are functioning properly, the conditional probability $\mathbf{P}(u/z_1, \ldots, z_n)$ is high.[10]

Like (15), (16) is a principle of trustworthiness – a principle of conditional reliability. Also like (15), it can play a useful role in explanations and can provide support for epistemological norms.

(12)–(16) are principles of reliability. In addition to the members of this family, there is also a principle concerning semantic correspondence that might be called a principle of success. This principle is concerned with the ways in which the semantic correlates of beliefs interact with the actions of an agent to enhance the chances that the agent's desires will be fulfilled. It runs as follows:

(17) Generally speaking, if it is the case (a) that $x$ is caused to perform an action $A$ by a desire $D$ and a plan involving a set of beliefs $B_1, \ldots, B_n$, (b) that $y_1, \ldots, y_n$ are the thoughts that serve as the propositional objects of $B_1, \ldots, B_n$, (c) that $y_1, \ldots, y_n$ correspond respectively to the states of affairs $z_1, \ldots, z_n$, (d) that the propositional object of $D$ corresponds semantically to the state of affairs $u$, and (e) that $w$ is the state of affairs that consists in $x$'s performing $A$, then, provided that $x$'s planning and decision-making faculties are functioning properly, the conditional probability $\mathbf{P}(u/z_1, \ldots, z_n, w)$ is higher than $\mathbf{P}(u)$.[11]

(17) owes its truth to several factors – to the world, to the nature of semantic correspondence, and to the fact that human planning and decision-making faculties tend to be highly effective, producing scenarios that provide for a variety of environmental contingencies and that are well grounded in perceptually acquired information. It is clear that it is a quite useful principle. Thus, among other things, it combines with principles like (12)–(16) to explain why human agents tend on the whole to be successful in attaining their goals.

In concluding this part of our discussion, I note that there is a family of principles that put the notion of semantic correspondence to use in specifying the extramental conditions under which desires are acquired and extinguished. One such principle is a commonsense variant of the principle that psychologists call the "Law of Effect." The principle that I have in mind can be formulated as follows:

(18) Generally speaking, if $N$ is a need such that in $x$'s experience instances of the property $\phi$ have consistently fulfilled $N$, then on those occasions when $N$ is particularly pressing and $x$'s perceptual state carries information to the

effect that there is an instance of φ in the current environment, $x$ forms a desire whose semantic correlate is a state of affairs involving $x$'s obtaining an instance of φ.

In short, the principle asserts that we tend to form desires for things that experience has shown to fulfill our needs.

We have found a set of principles which clearly attest to the theoretical utility of relational semantic concepts. It would, I think, be possible to continue to expand our list of such principles for some time. But to do so is probably unnecessary. It seems likely that (12)–(18) are sufficient to show that our relational semantic concepts are fully capable of earning their keep in the a posteriori regions of folk psychology, due to the roles they play in systematizing and deepening our understanding of how the mind interacts with the world. By the same token, it seems likely that they provide us with an adequate grasp of the fact that the laws of folk psychology *privilege* our relational concepts, giving us reasons to focus on semantic expression and semantic correspondence in preference to other concepts that stand for mind–world relations.

VI

In explaining and defending substitutionalism in Chapter 3, I maintained, in effect, that our relational semantic concepts are virtually thrust upon us by certain formal features of our practice of constructing canonical names for concepts and thoughts. The merits of this view are nicely illustrated by the case of semantic correspondence, which is more or less typical. Where $\langle x, y \rangle$ is any pair that falls within the extension of the concept of correspondence, there is a striking formal relationship between our canonical name for $x$ and our canonical name for $y$. Specifically, in the case of any such pair, it is true that our canonical name for $x$ has the form *the thought that p* and that our canonical name for $y$ has the form *the state of affairs that p*. Thus, the names are alike in that the thought content $p$ is their primary constituent. Because of the salience of this purely formal fact, we observed, it was virtually inevitable that the concept of semantic correspondence should find a place in our conceptual scheme.

In Chapter 3, then, there is a plausible explanation of why it is that we possess relational semantic concepts, an explanation that is based on formal features of canonical names. Now the task of explaining why it is that we possess the concepts in question is very different from the task of explaining why it is that we find them useful. In the present chapter,

I have attempted to discharge this second explanatory task, maintaining that the utility of relational concepts derives in part from the fact that they enhance the classificatory power of our conceptual scheme, and in part from the fact that they enable the formulation of generalizations about relationships between conceptually informed representations and constituents of extraconceptual reality. We are now in a position to say, I think, that in addition to being virtually inevitable, an involvement with relational concepts is extremely desirable.

In addition to the explicit themes of this chapter, there has also been an underlying concern – specifically, that of determining whether substitutionalism is compatible with the roles that relational concepts play in our thought. As we noted at the outset, if there are any features of our use of relational concepts that are incompatible with the substitutional accounts of those concepts that are offered in earlier chapters, those features would very likely come to light in the course of an examination of the factors that account for the utility of the concepts. For the use of a concept is generally determined by the factors that are responsible for the concept's utility. It appears, however, that substitutionalism is fully compatible with all of the data we have considered. Hence, while the lines of thought of the present chapter cannot be said to establish that substitutionalism squares with *all* of the relevant data (after all, there may be factors relevant to the utility of relational concepts that we have overlooked), it seems fair to think of those lines of thought as strengthening the case for substitutionalism.[12]

Furthermore, in addition to having found grounds for thinking that substitutionalism is logically compatible with the main facts concerning the utility of relational concepts, we can claim to have found grounds for thinking that substitutionalism actually predicts those facts. According to substitutionalism, relational semantic concepts can be explicitly defined in terms of substitutional quantifiers. It follows that if substitutionalism is true, then it should be the case that relational concepts supplement the expressive power of our conceptual scheme in the same ways as substitutional quantifiers. This prediction turns out to be correct. Thus, for example, as we observed in Section V, the notion of semantic correspondence enables us to formulate the following law:

(12) Generally speaking, if $x$ is an agent who comes to believe the thought $y$ as a result of perception, and $z$ is the state of affairs that semantically corresponds to $y$, then, provided that $x$'s perceptual mechanisms are functioning properly, $z$ is a distal cause of $x$'s belief.

Now the facts that are captured by (12) can also be captured by a generalization involving substitutional quantification. Thus, (12) is equivalent to (19):

(19) For any $x$, $(\Pi p)$(if $x$ is an agent who comes to believe the thought that $p$ as a result of perception, then, provided that $x$'s perceptual mechanisms are functioning properly, the state of affairs that $p$ is a distal cause of $x$'s belief).

But (12) is just one case. Can this observation be generalized? Is it generally true that the purposes served by propositions involving relational concepts can be served as well by propositions involving substitutional quantification? Reflection shows that the answer is "yes."[13]

# 6

## *Into the Wild Blue Yonder:* Nondesignating Concepts, Vagueness, Semantic Paradox, and Logical Paradox

There are a number of problems concerning our semantic concepts that a theory of truth must eventually face. I have discussed some of these problems in the foregoing pages, but nothing has been said thus far about two members of this category that are widely regarded as particularly important. I am unable to do justice to either of these problems in the present work, but it would be inappropriate to ignore them altogether. I must say what they are, explain how they interact with the main themes of the present work, and specify the obligations that they entail for someone who is concerned to develop those themes.

The first of these problems is the *problem of bivalence*. It arises from the fact that we have conflicting intuitions concerning the *law of bivalence* – that is, concerning the principle that every proposition is either true or false. Some of our intuitions appear to endorse this law. But we also have intuitions that appear to conflict with it. For example, where $P$ is any logically simple proposition containing a nondesignating singular concept, such as the proposition that Achilles was exactly six feet tall, we have a fairly strong inclination to deny that $P$ is true and also a fairly strong inclination to deny that $P$ is false. And the same applies to the members of several other categories of propositions. A theory of truth must somehow resolve the tension between the intuitions that appear to favor the law of bivalence and the intuitions that appear to oppose it.

The second problem is the *problem of the Liar*. Suppose that at time $t$ Ivan entertains the following thought:

The thought entertained by Ivan at time $t$ is not true.

This thought is the topic of the following derivations:

## Derivation I

(1) Suppose that the thought entertained by Ivan at time $t$ is true.     premise for conditional proof

(2) The thought entertained by Ivan at time $t$ = the thought that (the thought entertained by Ivan at time $t$ is not true).     premise

(3) The thought that (the thought entertained by Ivan at time $t$ is not true) is true if and only if the thought entertained by Ivan at time $t$ is not true.     premise

(4) The thought that (the thought entertained by Ivan at time $t$ is not true) is true.     (1), (2), substitution of identicals

(5) The thought entertained by Ivan at time $t$ is not true.     (3), (4), standard logic

(6) If the thought entertained by Ivan at time $t$ is true, then the thought entertained by Ivan at time $t$ is not true.     conditional proof

## Derivation II

(1) Suppose that the thought entertained by Ivan at time $t$ is not true.     premise for conditional proof

(2) The thought entertained by Ivan at time $t$ = the thought that (the thought entertained by Ivan at time $t$ is not true).     premise

(3) The thought that (the thought entertained by Ivan at time $t$ is not true) is true if and only if the thought entertained by Ivan at time $t$ is not true.     premise

(4) The thought that (the thought entertained by Ivan at time $t$ is not true) is not true.     (1), (2), substitution of identicals

(5) It's not the case that the    (3), (4), standard logic
thought entertained by Ivan
at time *t* is not true.

(6) The thought entertained by    (5), standard logic
Ivan at time *t* is true.

(7) If the thought entertained by    conditional proof
Ivan at time *t* is not true, then
the thought entertained by
Ivan at time *t* is true.

These derivations make use of two premises. One is the claim that the thought entertained by Ivan at time *t* = the thought that (the thought entertained by Ivan at time *t* is not true). We are obliged to accept this claim because, as a matter of empirical fact, Ivan did entertain the thought *the thought entertained by Ivan at time t is not true* at time *t*. The second premise, which appears as line (3) of each of the derivations, is an instance of our old friend, schema (T):

(T) The thought that *p* is true if and only if *p*.

Accordingly, it counts as analytic, for, as we have observed on several occasions, all instances of (T) are conceptually true. Thus, both of the premises of the foregoing derivations command our assent. But also, the various inferential steps strike us as entirely legitimate, being fully authorized by the laws of classical logic. It is clear, however, that *something* is wrong with the derivations, for their conclusions contradict one another.

The Liar Paradox arises in any conceptual scheme that satisfies three conditions: first, the scheme permits the construction of thoughts that are self-referential; second, the scheme enjoins conformity to the laws of classical logic; and third, the scheme carries a commitment to all propositions of form (T). It follows that the Liar poses a serious problem for *us*, for it is natural to suppose that *our* conceptual scheme satisfies all three of these conditions. Thus, we must ask: Is it *really* the case that our scheme generates arguments like Derivation I and Derivation II? If it is the case, then how can we best revise our scheme to avoid such contradictions? And if it is not the case, then why exactly do we find such derivations so seductive? To be complete, a theory of truth must deal with these questions in a fully satisfactory way.

II

As we noticed in the previous section, we have intuitions that strongly favor the law of bivalence, the principle that every proposition is either

111

true or false. Now, the substitutional theory of truth that is developed in earlier chapters is fully in accord with these intuitions. Indeed, when it is combined with a couple of plausible background assumptions, substitutionalism implies that the law of bivalence is an essential ingredient of our conceptual scheme. But this means that substitutionalism is challenged by the fact that we also have intuitions that appear to call the principle of bivalence into question.

To see that substitutionalism is in accord with the first set of intuitions, observe first that it is extremely plausible that we are committed to principles of deductive reasoning that incorporate the laws of classical logic. Because of this commitment, we are obliged to accept all propositions that count as instances of the law of excluded middle:

(EM) Either $p$ or it's not the case that $p$.

Second, observe that it is quite plausible that a thought counts as false if and only if its negation counts as true. That is to say, it is quite plausible that we are committed to accepting all instances of schema (F):

(F) The thought that $p$ is false if and only if the thought that it is not the case that $p$ is true.

Finally, recall that substitutionalism represents the conceptual scheme of common sense as a scheme that carries a commitment to principle (S):

(S) For any $x$, $x$ is true if and only if $(\Sigma p)((x = $ the thought that $p)$ and $p)$.

Now as we observed in Chapter 2, (S) supports derivations of instances of (T):

(T) The thought that $p$ is true if and only if $p$.

By the same token, it supports derivations of instances of (T$\star$):

(T$\star$) The thought that it is not the case that $p$ is true if and only if it is not the case that $p$.

Putting (EM) and (F) together with (T) and (T$\star$), we arrive at schema (B):

(B) Either the thought that $p$ is true or the thought that $p$ is false.

Thus, in combination with a couple of extremely plausible background claims, substitutionalism implies that the conceptual scheme of common sense carries a commitment to all instances of (B). But to say this is tantamount to saying that substitutionalism represents us as committed to the law of bivalence.

Now as we noticed earlier, we have a strong inclination to say that the following proposition is neither true nor false:

Achilles was exactly six feet tall.

And we have similar inclinations concerning other propositions that contain nondesignating singular concepts. How *could* such a proposition have a truth value, we find it natural to ask, when there is nothing in the world that is capable of making it true or making it false? Of course, to ask this question is to distance oneself from the law of bivalence.

In addition to our doubts about the bivalence of propositions with nondesignating singular concepts, we have doubts about the bivalence of normative propositions – or at least, we can be led to have them by reflecting on the difference between such propositions and propositions that make empirical claims. Thus, for example, when we consider the proposition that stealing is wrong in relation to the proposition that there are some very tall buildings in New York, we sense a deep difference that we are inclined to express by saying that the former proposition is neither true nor false. This perception parallels the perception about the *sentence* "Stealing is wrong" that Ayer expresses in the following well known passage:

The presence of an ethical symbol in a [sentence] adds nothing to its factual content. Thus, if I say to someone, "You acted wrongly in stealing that money," I am not stating anything more than if I had simply said, "You stole that money." In adding that this action is wrong I am not making any further statement about it. I am simply evincing my moral disapproval of it. . . . If I now generalize my previous statement and say, "Stealing is wrong," I produce a sentence which has no factual meaning . . . . It is clear that there is nothing said here which can be true or false.[1]

It is worth noting that the source of our doubts about the bivalence of normative propositions closely parallels the source of our doubts about the bivalence of propositions that contain nondesignating singular concepts. When we question the bivalence of the latter propositions, we do so because of the reflection that there are no entities in the world that are capable of *making* such propositions true or of *making* them false. It appears that we have similar perceptions about normative propositions. Thus, we are strongly inclined to question the idea that normative concepts can be said to stand for real properties. Can there really be such things as goodness and beauty in the world, we are inclined to ask? But if goodness and beauty do not exist in the realm of extraconceptual fact, then there is nothing in that realm that is capable of conferring truth or falsity on propositions that contain the concept of goodness and the concept of beauty.

There are several other categories of propositions that can reasonably be seen as exceptions to bivalence. Here I will just mention one other group – propositions that apply vague concepts to "borderline cases." In addition to the men who are clear cases of baldness, there are also men who resemble such paradigms to a fairly high degree but who do not count as definitely bald. Where $a$ is such a man, it is extremely tempting to deny that the proposition that $a$ is bald is true and also to deny that the proposition is false. Interestingly, it appears that our reservations about viewing such propositions as bivalent may have a different explanation than the corresponding reservations about propositions with nondesignating singular concepts and about normative propositions. Thus, we do not feel a strong temptation to deny objective existence to baldness. On the contrary, if $b$ is a paradigm of baldness, we are strongly inclined to say that $b$ has a real property – a property that distinguishes him determinately from many other individuals. Evidently, the intuitions that run counter to bivalence are a variegated lot, and it will not be easy to find a theoretical framework that describes and explains them.

Before completing this survey of the problem of bivalence, we should take note of a further complication. At the end of Chapter 3, we observed that there are situations in which we find it natural to make use of the concept of truth in connection with propositions that cannot be said to correspond semantically to states of affairs. Thus, even if one thinks that normative concepts fail to express real properties, one may still find it desirable and even necessary to endorse the proposition that all of Gandhi's moral views are true. Evidently, when we express the insight that the members of certain categories of propositions lack truth values, we are saying something that needs to be interpreted. We do not mean to be saying that it is absolutely inappropriate to think of the propositions in question as neither true nor false. We are making a point of some kind when we say such things, but there are grounds for doubting that we should be taken literally.

To summarize: We have intuitions that strongly favor the law of bivalence. Substitutionalism endorses these intuitions and explains why we have them, crediting us with conceptual structures that enjoin acceptance of the law. On the other hand, we also have intuitions that favor the view that there are several categories of propositions whose members are neither true nor false. These intuitions can be quite vivid, though it is probably not true that they should be accepted at face value in all cases.

I cannot hope to do justice to the problem of bivalence within the confines of the present work. The task of investigating it systematically will have to be left as a project for the future. But it is worth mentioning that there is a doctrine in the foregoing pages that seems at least to reduce the size of the problem. This is the doctrine that we are in possession of a concept of *truth conditions* according to which a thought counts as having a truth condition just in case it can be said to correspond semantically to a state of affairs. It seems entirely possible that when we deny that propositions with nondesignating singular concepts are bivalent, and when we make the corresponding claim about propositions that contain normative concepts, what we mean can be expressed more accurately by saying that they cannot be said to have truth conditions in this robust sense of "truth conditions." On this view, such denials of bivalence should not be taken literally, and they are therefore ultimately consistent both with a commitment to the law of bivalence and with claims like the claim that all of Gandhi's moral beliefs were true.

It is, of course, entirely natural to deny that propositions with nondesignating singular concepts have truth conditions in the sense of corresponding to an extramental state of affairs. Furthermore, from the perspective represented by the foregoing quotation from Ayer, it is also natural to deny that propositions that contain normative concepts have truth conditions of this robust sort.[2]

Perhaps it will be useful to restate the present proposal in somewhat different terms. As the reader will recall, at the end of Chapter 3 we accepted the claim (1) that we are in possession of a robust notion of truth conditions according to which a thought has truth conditions just in case it corresponds semantically to an extraconceptual state of affairs, and also the claim (2) that our core concept of truth is definitionally independent of this notion, with the result that it is entirely appropriate to attribute truth to a proposition while denying that the proposition has truth conditions in this robust sense. The present proposal simply spells out the implications of these conclusions for the problem posed by propositions that contain nondesignating concepts. According to the proposal, such propositions lack robust truth conditions because they fail to correspond semantically to extraconceptual states of affairs. But this fact fails to show that such propositions are neither true nor false. It could only show this if there were a definitional connection between the notion of truth and the robust notion of truth conditions. And (2) tells us that these notions are definitionally independent.

To keep the ledger straight, I should emphasize here that the present work credits us with two notions of truth conditions. One is the robust notion that we have just been considering. We have this notion, apparently, because in the overwhelming majority of cases that come to our attention, the propositions that we wish to classify as true or false can be said to correspond semantically to states of affairs. The other notion is much less substantial. This is the notion that we have in mind when we say that an agent can know the truth condition of a proposition simply in virtue of grasping the instance of (T) in which the proposition figures as a constituent. It appears to be possible to do full justice to this notion by saying that the truth conditions that it recognizes are simply *identical* with instances of (T).

It should also be emphasized that the present proposal is at best a partial solution to the problem of bivalence. It may help with those components of the problem that involve either nondesignating singular concepts or normative concepts. As we noticed, however, the component that involves vague concepts seems to require separate treatment. My own view is that the solution to this component of the problem requires advances in our understanding of vagueness rather than advances in our understanding of truth, but the task of defending this view lies well beyond the scope of the present work.

III

As we observed in Section I, the Liar Paradox arises within any conceptual scheme that permits the construction of self-referential thoughts, that endorses classical logic, and that enjoins acceptance of all instances of schema (T). Now it is quite plausible that the conceptual scheme of common sense satisfies the first two of these conditions. But also, as we observed in each of the previous two sections, substitutionalism represents that conceptual scheme as carrying a commitment to all instances of (T). It follows that if substitutionalism is true, then it is very likely the case that the scheme of common sense supports the construction of arguments like Derivation I and Derivation II.

Actually, the doctrines of the present work represent Liar-like phenomena as arising at an even deeper level. Thus, given the rules of inference that were used to explain substitutional quantification in Chapter 2, it is possible to construct paradoxical arguments without making use of instances of schema (T). In other words, contradictions can be shown to follow *directly* from the logical framework that substitutionalism attributes to our conceptual scheme. The route to contradiction that leads through semantic principles is a detour.

To elaborate: As the reader may recall, the rules governing the substitutional quantifiers run as follows:

*Universal Elimination*

$$\frac{(\Pi \mathbf{p})(\ldots \mathbf{p} \ldots)}{(\ldots T \ldots)} \qquad \frac{(\Pi \mathbf{p})(\ldots \mathbf{p} \ldots)}{(\ldots \mathbf{q} \ldots)}$$

Here $T$ is a particular, determinate thought, and $(\ldots T \ldots)$ is the particular, determinate thought that comes from replacing all free occurrences of the propositional variable $\mathbf{p}$ in the open thought $(\ldots \mathbf{p} \ldots)$ with $T$. Further, $\mathbf{q}$ is a propositional variable, and $(\ldots \mathbf{q} \ldots)$ is the open thought that comes from replacing all free occurrences of the propositional variable $\mathbf{p}$ in the open thought $(\ldots \mathbf{p} \ldots)$ with free occurrences of $\mathbf{q}$.

*Universal Introduction*

$$\frac{(\ldots \mathbf{q} \ldots)}{(\Pi \mathbf{p})(\ldots \mathbf{p} \ldots)}$$

Here $\mathbf{q}$ is a propositional variable, and $(\ldots \mathbf{q} \ldots)$ is the open thought that comes from replacing all free occurrences of the propositional variable $\mathbf{p}$ in the open thought $(\ldots \mathbf{p} \ldots)$ with free occurrences of $\mathbf{q}$. Further, for Universal Introduction to be performed properly, $\mathbf{q}$ must satisfy two additional conditions: (i) $\mathbf{q}$ must not have a free occurrence in the thought $(\Pi \mathbf{p})(\ldots \mathbf{p} \ldots)$; and (ii) $\mathbf{q}$ must not have a free occurrence in any premise on which $(\Pi \mathbf{p})(\ldots \mathbf{p} \ldots)$ depends.

*Existential Introduction*

$$\frac{(\ldots T \ldots)}{(\Sigma \mathbf{p})(\ldots \mathbf{p} \ldots)} \qquad \frac{(\ldots \mathbf{q} \ldots)}{(\Sigma \mathbf{p})(\ldots \mathbf{p} \ldots)}$$

Here $T$ is a particular, determinate thought, and $(\ldots T \ldots)$ is the particular, determinate thought that comes from replacing all free occurrences of the propositional variable $\mathbf{p}$ in the open thought $(\ldots \mathbf{p} \ldots)$ with $T$. Further, $\mathbf{q}$ is a propositional variable, and $(\ldots \mathbf{q} \ldots)$ is the open thought that comes from replacing all

free occurrences of the propositional variable **p** in the open thought
(...**p**...) with free occurrences of **q**.

*Existential Elimination*

$(\Sigma\mathbf{p})(\ldots \mathbf{p} \ldots)$

$\dfrac{\text{If}(\ldots \mathbf{q} \ldots), \text{ then } T}{T}$

Here $T$ is a thought, **q** is a propositional variable, and (...**q**...) is
the open thought that comes from replacing all free occurrences of
the propositional variable **p** in the open thought (... **p**...) with free
occurrences of **q**. Further, for Existential Elimination to be properly
performed, **q** must satisfy three additional conditions: (i) it cannot
have a free occurrence in $T$; (ii) it cannot have a free occurrence
in $(\Sigma\mathbf{p})(\ldots \mathbf{p}\ldots)$; and (iii) it cannot have a free occurrence in any
premise on which the thought $T$ depends.

Alas, a little reflection shows that these rules are dangerous! Suppose, for
example, that at time $t$ Jane entertains the following thought:

$(\Sigma p)$((the thought that Jane entertains at time $t =$ the thought that $p$) and it's not
the case that $p$).

As is shown in the Appendix, it is possible to use the rules of inference
given above to construct derivations of the following two claims about
this thought:

(JANE1) If $(\Sigma p)$((the thought that Jane entertains at time $t =$ the thought that $p$)
and $p$), then it's not the case that $(\Sigma p)$((the thought that Jane entertains
at time $t =$ the thought that $p$) and $p$).

(JANE2) If it's not the case that $(\Sigma p)$((the thought that Jane entertains at time $t =$
the thought that $p$) and $p$), then $(\Sigma p)$((the thought that Jane entertains
at time $t =$ the thought that $p$) and $p$).

Unfortunately, (JANE1) and (JANE2) are contradictory. It turns out,
then, that in claiming that the foregoing rules of inference are embedded
in our conceptual scheme, substitutionalism represents our conceptual
scheme as incoherent. And it does so quite independently of the account
of truth that it derives from this substitutional infrastructure. It represents
our scheme as incoherent in its logical core.

We can summarize these findings by saying that substitutionalism is
committed to the *incoherence thesis* – that is, to the claim that our conceptual

scheme has basic structural features which permit the derivation of contradictions. Now this conclusion might seem to be a reason for setting
substitutionalism aside and pursuing some other version of deflationism
in its stead. In fact, however, there is good reason to think that it is impossible to construct a satisfactory account of our intuitive concept of
truth that is not committed to the incoherence thesis. Thus, as we have
noted with some frequency in the preceding pages, it is overwhelmingly
plausible that our intuitive conception of truth is constitutively linked to
the instances of schema (T). To be more specific, it is overwhelmingly
plausible that if an agent possesses the concept of truth, then he or she is
disposed to recognize every processable instance of (T) as having a claim
upon his or her assent. In view of this fact, it is overwhelmingly plausible
that any theory that is concerned to *describe* our conceptual scheme, as
opposed to being concerned to reform it, will inevitably be committed
to the incoherence thesis.

Alfred Tarski came to a similar conclusion, though he preferred to state
his view as a claim about natural language. Referring to the semantic
paradoxes, Tarski wrote that they "prove emphatically that the concept
of truth (as well as other semantic concepts) when applied to colloquial
language in conjunction with the normal laws of logic leads inevitably to
confusions and contradictions."[3] Several other authors have ratified this
claim.[4]

It appears, however, that most philosophers have been shocked by
Tarski's version of the incoherence thesis, and have thought it necessary
to reject it. And they have had a point. After all, the incoherence thesis can appear to entail that we are obliged to accept every proposition
whatsoever. (Thus, where *P* is any proposition whatsoever, it is possible
to use classical logic to construct a derivation leading from a contradiction
to *P*.) But if we are obliged to accept *every* proposition, there can be no
distinction between warranted belief and folly! Thus, it can seem that the
incoherence thesis entails the claim that we are unable to draw even the
most elementary epistemological distinctions. It is clear, however, that
this claim misrepresents our epistemological situation. Even after we have
been exposed to the semantic paradoxes, we are perfectly capable of distinguishing between sound doctrine and error – or at least, we are capable
of drawing such distinctions in favorable circumstances.

While acknowledging the prima facie force of this argument, I wish to
maintain that the incoherence thesis is in the end compatible with a proper
appreciation of our actual epistemological situation. The thesis need not
be thought to entail that we are irreversibly committed to embracing all

of the propositions that we recognize as having a special claim on our assent. In fact, as we all know, our commitments are generally qualified and provisional – even when they are deeply rooted. As it is understood here, the incoherence thesis reflects this fundamental fact. It recognizes that we are capable of bracketing or deactivating a commitment when it becomes impossible to honor it.

To elaborate: Let us suppose that a certain agent, Fred, has just become aware of the semantic paradoxes (or of the paradoxical result presented in the Appendix), and let us suppose that he has decided to accept the view that the paradoxes are not illusions, but rather flow from the basic structure of his conceptual scheme. Furthermore, let us suppose that Fred continues to be aware that the relevant portions of his conceptual scheme have inestimable practical and theoretical utility. And finally, let us suppose that Fred feels that, for the time being at least, he is unable to revise his scheme in such a way as to retain its benefits while eliminating the attendant risks. Is this situation impossible? Is Fred unable to distinguish between right opinion and error? It seems not. If Fred finds that a rule leads to a contradiction when it is applied to a particular proposition, he can simply withdraw that application of the rule, pleading in justification that endorsement of the application would lead to a disaster. (By "disaster" I mean a leveling of principles and distinctions that Fred has found useful in other contexts.) It seems that a policy of proceeding in this way would be entirely workable. But also, given our assumptions about Fred's epistemic situation, it would appear that such a policy would be fully rational, provided that it was combined with a commitment, on Fred's part, to continue to seek a satisfactory revision of his conceptual scheme.

It appears, then, that we should accept the incoherence thesis and commit ourselves to searching for a satisfactory revision of our conceptual scheme – that is, a revision that blocks the derivation of the Liar Paradox and also the derivation of all related semantic and logical antinomies. The present work is concerned only with descriptive questions about the structure of our actual conceptual scheme, so the task of seeking an acceptable revision lies far outside its scope. But I note with pleasure and anticipation that the contemporary literature on the Liar contains a number of promising proposals.[5] Generally speaking, these proposals can be adapted to yield programs for revising the substitutional logic that is formulated above in such a way as to block the derivation of contradictions. Accordingly, while it is necessary for the present to accommodate to the fact that there are pockets of semantic and logical incoherence in our conceptual scheme, there is reason to hope that in the not too distant future we will be in a position to describe these pockets exhaustively, and to take well motivated steps to eliminate them.

## APPENDIX

In this appendix, I construct derivations of the following two propositions:

(JANE1) If $(\Sigma p)$((the thought that Jane entertains at time $t =$ the thought that $p$) and $p$), then it's not the case that $(\Sigma p)$((the thought that Jane entertains at time $t =$ the thought that $p$) and $p$).

(JANE2) If it's not the case that $(\Sigma p)$((the thought that Jane entertains at time $t =$ the thought that $p$) and $p$), then $(\Sigma p)$((the thought that Jane entertains at time $t =$ the thought that $p$) and $p$).

I will need only two background assumptions, viz.:

(I) $(\Pi p)(\Pi q)$(if the thought that $p =$ the thought that $q$, then $p$ if and only if $q$).
(II) The thought that Jane entertains at time $t =$ the thought that $(\Sigma p)$((the thought that Jane entertains at time $t =$ the thought that $p$) and it's not the case that $p$).

(I) can be seen to be correct by reflection, and (II) is shown to be correct by the empirical facts involving Jane's stream of thought.

I will use the symbol $\sim$ to abbreviate negation, and will at two points make use of the logical principle that propositions of form (a) can be interchanged in all contexts with propositions of form (b):

(a) $(\sim \Sigma \mathbf{p})(\dots \mathbf{p} \dots)$
(b) $(\Pi \mathbf{p}) \sim (\dots \mathbf{p} \dots)$.

This principle can be justified by the standard rules of inference for negation and the rules for the substitutional quantifiers that are given in the text. I will call it the *principle of interchange*.

### Derivation III

(1) $(\Sigma p)$((the thought that Jane entertains at time $t =$ the thought that $p$) and $p$).     premise for conditional proof

(2) (the thought that Jane entertains at time $t =$ the thought that $p$) and $p$.     premise for conditional proof

(3) The thought that Jane entertains at time $t =$ the thought that $(\Sigma p)((\text{the thought that Jane entertains at time } t = \text{the thought that } p) \text{ and } \sim p)$.    (II)

(4) The thought that $p =$ the thought that $(\Sigma p)((\text{the thought that Jane entertains at time } t = \text{the thought that } p) \text{ and } \sim p)$.    (2), (3), substitutivity of identity

(5) $(\Pi p)(\Pi q)(\text{if the thought that } p = \text{the thought that } q, \text{ then } p \text{ if and only if } q)$.    (I)

(6) If the thought that $p =$ the thought that $(\Sigma p)((\text{the thought that Jane entertains at time } t = \text{the thought that } p) \text{ and } \sim p)$, then $p$ if and only if $(\Sigma p)((\text{the thought that Jane entertains at time } t = \text{the thought that } p) \text{ and } \sim p)$.    (5), Universal Elimination

(7) $p$ if and only if $(\Sigma p)((\text{the thought that Jane entertains at time } t = \text{the thought that } p) \text{ and } \sim p)$.    (4), (6) standard logic

(8) $(\Sigma p)((\text{the thought that Jane entertains at time } t = \text{the thought that } p) \text{ and } \sim p)$.    (2), (8) standard logic

(9) (the thought that Jane entertains at time $t =$ the thought that $q$) and $\sim q$.    premise for conditional proof

(10) The thought that $p =$ the thought that $q$.    (2), (9), standard logic

(11) If the thought that $p =$ the thought that $q$, then $p$ if and only if $q$.    (5), Universal Elimination

(12) $p$ if and only if $q$.    (10), (11), standard logic

(13) $\sim p$.    (9), (12), standard logic

(14) $p$ and $\sim p$.    (2), (13), standard logic

(15) $\sim(\Sigma p)((\text{the thought that Jane entertains at time } t = \text{the thought that } p) \text{ and } p)$.    (14), standard logic (ex falso quodlibet)

(16) If (the thought that Jane entertains at time $t = $ the thought that $q$) and $\sim q$, then $\sim(\Sigma p)((\text{the thought that Jane entertains at time } t = \text{the thought that } p)$ and $p)$.     (9)–(15), conditional proof

(17) $\sim(\Sigma p)((\text{the thought that Jane entertains at time } t = \text{the thought that } p)$ and $p)$.     (8), (16), Existential Elimination

(18) If (the thought that Jane entertains at time $t = $ the thought that $p$) and $p$, then $\sim(\Sigma p)((\text{the thought that Jane entertains at time } t = \text{the thought that } p)$ and $p)$.     (2)–(17), conditional proof

(19) $\sim(\Sigma p)((\text{the thought that Jane entertains at time } t = \text{the thought that } p)$ and $p)$.     (1), (18), Existential Elimination

(20) If $(\Sigma p)((\text{the thought that Jane entertains at time } t = \text{the thought that } p)$ and $p)$, then $\sim(\Sigma p)((\text{the thought that Jane entertains at time } t = \text{the thought that } p)$ and $p)$.     (1)–(19), conditional proof

## Derivation IV

(1) $\sim(\Sigma p)((\text{the thought that Jane entertains at time } t = \text{the thought that } p)$ and $p)$.     premise for conditional proof

(2) $(\Pi p)(\text{if the thought that Jane entertains at time } t = \text{the thought that } p, \text{ then } \sim p)$.     (1), principle of interchange, standard logic

(3) If the thought that Jane entertains at time $t = $ the thought that $(\Sigma p)((\text{the thought that Jane entertains at time } t = \text{the thought that } p)$ and $\sim p)$, then $\sim(\Sigma p)((\text{the thought that Jane entertains at time } t = \text{the thought that } p)$ and $\sim p)$.     (2), Universal Elimination

123

(4) The thought that Jane entertains at time $t$ = the thought that $(\Sigma p)$((the thought that Jane entertains at time $t$ = the thought that $p$) and $\sim p$).　(II)

(5) $\sim(\Sigma p)$((the thought that Jane entertains at time $t$ = the thought that $p$) and $\sim p$).　(3), (4), standard logic

(6) $(\Pi p)$(if the thought that Jane entertains at time $t$ = the thought that $p$, then $p$).　(5), principle of interchange, standard logic

(7) If the thought that Jane entertains at time $t$ = the thought that $(\Sigma p)$((the thought that Jane entertains at time $t$ = the thought that $p$) and $\sim p$), then $(\Sigma p)$((the thought that Jane entertains at time $t$ = the thought that $p$) and $\sim p$).　(6), Universal Elimination

(8) $(\Sigma p)$((the thought that Jane entertains at time $t$ = the thought that $p$) and $\sim p$).　(4), (7), standard logic

(9) $\sim(\Sigma p)$((the thought that Jane entertains at time $t$ = the thought that $p$) and $\sim p$) and $(\Sigma p)$((the thought that Jane entertains at time $t$ = the thought that $p$) and $\sim p$).　(5), (8), standard logic

(10) $(\Sigma p)$((the thought that Jane entertains at time $t$ = the thought that $p$) and $p$).　(9), standard logic (*ex falso quodibet*)

(11) If $\sim(\Sigma p)$((the thought that Jane entertains at time $t$ = the thought that $p$) and $p$), then $(\Sigma p)$((the thought that Jane entertains at time $t$ = the thought that $p$) and $p$).　(1)–(10), conditional proof

Elimination represents the natural way of generalizing the principle of constructive dilemma.

To be sure, there is a way of changing the foregoing rules while preserving their basic structural similarity to the rules that govern disjunction. Thus, it is possible to modify them by simply introducing qualifications into the explanations and restrictions that follow the rules. Consider, for example, the stipulation "Here $T$ is [any] particular, determinate thought." (Cf. the foregoing formulation of Existential Introduction.) It is easy to imagine alterations to this stipulation that would block derivations like Derivation III and Derivation IV. We could, for example, replace it with the more restrictive stipulation that runs as follows: "Here $T$ is any particular, determinate thought *that does not itself contain a substitutional quantifier.*" This revision would effectively block the foregoing derivations. Moreover, it would do so while preserving the basic structure of Existential Introduction and the basic structure of Existential Elimination.

Unfortunately, in addition to their respective individual vices (which tend to be serious), all such proposals fail to do justice to the intended meanings of $(\Sigma p)$ and $(\Pi p)$. To see this, observe that if we were to embrace the revised stipulation in the preceding paragraph, we would be obliged to view $(\Sigma p)$ as equivalent to the restricted quantifier *for some p such that the thought that p contains no substitutional quantifiers*, and we would be forced to view $(\Pi p)$ as equivalent to the restricted quantifier *for every p such that the thought that p contains no substitutional quantifiers.* This would, of course, preclude our viewing them as equivalent respectively to *for some p* and *for all p*. And by the same token, it would preclude our using them to model the logical behavior of intuitive substitutional quantifiers like the ones that we considered in Chapter 2, for those quantifiers (e.g., *without fail*) count intuitively as being altogether unrestricted.

In view of these derivations, we are obliged to conclude that the foregoing rules of inference for the substitutional quantifiers permit the derivation of contradictions. Would it be possible to avoid this result by modifying the rules? Well, yes. It is clear, however, that a modification would have to cut quite deep, for it is clear that the foregoing rules are forced upon us by the fact that $(\Sigma p)$ and $(\Pi p)$ are being used respectively to abbreviate *for some p* and *for all p*. Consider, for example, the first of these quantifiers. It is quite clear that we are obliged to suppose that it satisfies a principle like Existential Introduction, for Existential Introduction is equivalent to the principle that it is always permissible to infer a proposition of the form *(for some p)(. . . p . . .)* from any substitution instance of that proposition. What could be more evident? Furthermore, reflection shows that we are obliged to suppose that $(\Sigma p)$ satisfies a principle like Existential Elimination, for Existential Elimination is equivalent to the following rule: if it is possible to derive a proposition $T$ from a schema which represents the *common form* and *common content* of *all* substitution instances of a proposition of the form *(for some p)(. . . p . . .)*, then it is permissible to infer $T$ from the latter proposition itself. Again, what could be more obviously correct?

These observations can be reformulated as follows: The quantifier $(\Sigma p)$ is a kind of generalized disjunction. Accordingly, in choosing rules of inference to capture its role in our thought, it is necessary to choose rules that are as similar as possible to the introduction and elimination rules that govern the concept of disjunction. Now, as many philosophers and logicians have observed, the most natural introduction rules for disjunction are the following:

$$\frac{p}{p \text{ or } q} \qquad \frac{q}{p \text{ or } q}$$

Moreover, the most natural elimination rule for disjunction is the principle that is known as *constructive dilemma* – that is, the principle which authorizes the inference of a proposition from a disjunction if the proposition can be shown to follow from each of the relevant disjuncts. It follows from these observations that Existential Introduction and Existential Elimination are the right rules for the substitutional quantifier $(\Sigma p)$. Thus, Existential Introduction represents the natural way of generalizing the foregoing introduction rules for disjunction, and Existential

66

kind concepts are also sortal concepts – *rabbit* is an example, and so are *grain of sand, raindrop, tree,* and *finger.* Like all observational kind concepts, observational kind concepts that are sortals satisfy (7) and (8). But they also satisfy an additional principle that runs as follows:

(9) Let C be a sortal kind concept that expresses a property φ, and let φ be a sortal kind that is observationally accessible. Under these assumptions, if x is an agent who possesses C, then it must be the case that x satisfies the following condition: x is disposed to use C in observationally grounded individuative judgments that reflect the spatiotemporal boundaries of instances of φ.

There are a number of ways in which judgments can reflect the spatiotemporal boundaries of objects, but it will suffice for our purposes to mention a couple. So, in the first place: Suppose that an agent is disposed to accept thoughts of the form *this rabbit is white* when and only when he or she is confronted with a rabbit whose surface is entirely white (so that, for example, the agent will not accept a thought of the given form when an otherwise black rabbit has a white spot on its side). Such an agent is disposed to make judgments that reflect the spatial boundaries of rabbits.[7] Second: Suppose that an agent is disposed to accept thoughts of the form *this rabbit is identical with that rabbit* when and only when these conditions are satisfied: (a) his or her use of the demonstrative concept *this rabbit* is temporarily controlled by perceptual information about a certain rabbit $r_1$; (b) his or her use of the demonstrative concept *that rabbit* is temporarily controlled by perceptual information about a certain rabbit $r_2$; and (c) $r_1$ is identical with $r_2$. Such is an agent whose judgments reflect the spatial boundaries of rabbits and also their temporal boundaries.[8,9]

In addition to generalizations that are concerned exclusively with kind concepts, there are others that are concerned with concepts of quite different sorts. Thus, in the first place, Kripke's work suggests that there is a variant of (7) that applies to an enormous range of concepts that stand for individual substances. To be more specific, Kripke's work suggests that something like the following is true: If an agent possesses a nominal concept that refers to a spatiotemporal particular, then it must be the case that the agent's acquisition of the concept was shaped by causal traces of the particular – for example, by utterances of other agents that were themselves due, ultimately, to states of affairs involving the particular. (As in the case of (7), I am simplifying here by prescinding from cases in which agents possess concepts in virtue of having fixed their reference with descriptions that are known on independent grounds to refer.) Furthermore, it appears that there are variants of (7) and (8) which apply to general concepts that express *theoretical* natural kinds – that is, to concepts such as *hydrogen atom* and *black hole*. Of course, principles that are concerned with concepts that express theoretical kinds could not speak of direct perceptual interactions between agents and samples of kinds. Rather, they will be concerned with perceptual interactions between agents and experimental traces of samples of kinds. Apart from this difference, however, the relevant principles will be quite similar to (7) and (8). Finally, it is plausible that there is a variant of (9) that applies to theoretical sortal concepts.

It appears, then, that the family of principles that includes (7), (8), and (9) is quite large, and that it has implications concerning all concepts that stand for spatiotemporal entities. But this is not the end of the story. There are also principles which apply to concepts that designate various sorts of abstract entity. I will illustrate this with an example involving an important class of arithmetical concepts. To appreciate the example, observe that arithmetical concepts appear to fall into three categories: There are concepts that we possess in virtue of having accepted explicit definitions, concepts that we possess in virtue of having accepted implicit definitions, and concepts that we possess in virtue of having mastered computational procedures. My example is concerned with concepts that belong to the third category – specifically, with concepts that count as *computational*. It can be formulated as follows:

(10) Let C be a computational arithmetical concept that stands for a dyadic arithmetical function **f**. Given this assumption, if x possesses C, then it must be the case that x possesses a computational procedure P involving C such that P satisfies the following condition: If P were realized in an "ideal agent" (i.e., an agent with unlimited working memory and computation time), and the agent applied P to the numerical concepts m and n, then P would cause the agent to believe the thought $mCn = p$ if and only if, where w, y and z are the natural numbers that serve as the referents of m, n, and p, respectively, z is the number that results when the function **f** is applied to w and y.

In effect, (10) tells us that if x possesses a computational concept that stands for a dyadic arithmetical function, then x must possess a computational procedure which, if realized in an ideal agent, would lead that agent to make elementary numerical judgments involving that concept in such a way as to mirror the elementary facts in which that function is involved. Or, to adapt a piece of jargon from metamathematics, x's use of the tantamount to saying that substitutionalism represents us as committed to the law of bivalence.

Now as we noticed earlier, we have a strong inclination to say that the following proposition is neither true nor false:

Achilles was exactly six feet tall.

And we have similar inclinations concerning other propositions that contain nondesignating singular concepts. How *could* such a proposition have a truth value, we find it natural to ask, when there is nothing in the world that is capable of making it true or making it false? Of course, to ask this question is to distance oneself from the law of bivalence.

In addition to our doubts about the bivalence of propositions with nondesignating singular concepts, we have doubts about the bivalence of normative propositions – or at least, we can be led to have them by reflecting on the difference between such propositions and propositions that make empirical claims. Thus, for example, when we consider the proposition that stealing is wrong in relation to the proposition that there are some very tall buildings in New York, we sense a deep difference that we are inclined to express by saying that the former proposition is neither true nor false. This perception parallels the perception about the *sentence* "Stealing is wrong" that Ayer expresses in the following well known passage:

The presence of an ethical symbol in a [sentence] adds nothing to its factual content. Thus, if I say to someone, "You acted wrongly in stealing that money," I am not stating anything more than if I had simply said, "You stole that money." In adding that this action is wrong I am not making any further statement about it. I am simply evincing my moral disapproval of it.... If I now generalize my previous statement and say, "Stealing is wrong," I produce a sentence which has no factual meaning.... It is clear that there is nothing said here which can be true or false.[1]

It is worth noting that the source of our doubts about the bivalence of normative propositions closely parallels the source of our doubts about the bivalence of propositions that contain nondesignating singular concepts. When we question the bivalence of the latter propositions, we do so because of the reflection that there are no entities in the world that are capable of *making* such propositions true or of *making* them false. It appears that we have similar perceptions about normative propositions. Thus, we are strongly inclined to question the idea that normative concepts can be said to stand for real properties. Can there really be such things as

113

goodness and beauty in the world, we are inclined to ask? But if goodness and beauty do not exist in the realm of extraconceptual fact, then there is nothing in that realm that is capable of conferring truth or falsity on propositions that contain the concept of goodness and the concept of beauty.

There are several other categories of propositions that can reasonably be seen as exceptions to bivalence. Here I will just mention one other group – propositions that apply vague concepts to "borderline cases." In addition to the men who are clear cases of baldness, there are also men who resemble such paradigms to a fairly high degree but who do not count as definitely bald. Where $a$ is such a man, it is extremely tempting to deny that the proposition that $a$ is bald is true and also to deny that the proposition is false. Interestingly, it appears that our reservations about viewing such propositions as bivalent may have a different explanation than the corresponding reservations about propositions with nondesignating singular concepts and about normative propositions. Thus, we do not feel a strong temptation to deny objective existence to baldness. On the contrary, if $b$ is a paradigm of baldness, we are strongly inclined to say that $b$ has a real property – a property that distinguishes him determinately from many other individuals. Evidently, the intuitions that run counter to bivalence are a variegated lot, and it will not be easy to find a theoretical framework that describes and explains them.

Before completing this survey of the problem of bivalence, we should take note of a further complication. At the end of Chapter 3, we observed that there are situations in which we find it natural to make use of the concept of truth in connection with propositions that cannot be said to correspond semantically to states of affairs. Thus, even if one thinks that normative concepts fail to express real properties, one may still find it desirable and even necessary to endorse the proposition that all of Gandhi's moral views are true. Evidently, when we express the insight that the members of certain categories of propositions lack truth values, we are saying something that needs to be interpreted. We do not mean to be saying that it is absolutely inappropriate to think of the propositions in question as neither true nor false. We are making a point of some kind when we say such things, but there are grounds for doubting that we should be taken literally.

To summarize: We have intuitions that strongly favor the law of bivalence. Substitutionalism endorses these intuitions and explains why we have them, crediting us with conceptual structures that enjoin acceptance of the law. On the other hand, we also have intuitions that favor the

# Notes

CHAPTER 1. INTRODUCTION

1. Herbert G. Macy and Bruce M. Metzger (eds.), *The New Oxford Annotated Bible*, revised standard version (New York: Oxford, 1973), p. 1314.

2. Here, in outline, is a typical defense: (1) When one uses the predicate "believes that $S$" to attribute a belief to someone, the embedded sentence $S$ indicates the proposition that serves as the object of the belief. (2) The proposition that $S$ indicates when it occurs in the predicate "believes that $S$" is the same as the proposition that $S$ expresses when it is used in other contexts. (3) It follows from (1) and (2) that if the predicates "believes that $S$" and "believes that $S^\star$" can be used to attribute different beliefs, then the propositions that are expressed by the sentences $S$ and $S^\star$ must be numerically distinct. (4) If there are any logical differences between $S$ and $S^\star$ (including even differences in logical microstructure), then the predicates "believes that $S$" and "believes that $S^\star$" can be used to express different beliefs. (5) It follows from (3) and (4) that propositions are distinct when the sentences that express them are different in point of logical form. (6) The best explanation of (5) is the hypothesis that propositions have internal logical structures that reflect the logical structures of the sentences that are used to express them. Hence, by (5) and (6), the hypothesis that propositions have internal logical structures that reflect the structures of sentences is correct.

Step (4) in this argument is richly supported by semantic intuitions. It is pretty clear, for example, that the predicate "believes that there could be a set x such that x has as members all and only those sets that are not members of themselves" can be used to attribute a different belief than the predicate "believes that there could be a set x such that (i) x has as members all and only those sets that are not members of themselves and (ii) x both has itself as a member and fails to have itself as a member." But the two embedded sentences are logically equivalent and alike in point of conceptual constituents. They differ only in point of logical structure.

For further discussion, see the essays in Nathan Salmon and Scott Soames (eds.), *Propositions and Attitudes* (Oxford: Oxford University Press, 1988).

3. This use of the term "thought" is fairly standard in large portions of the philosophical literature, including especially those portions that are either concerned with or influenced by Fregean doctrines about meaning. See the writings collected in Max Black and Peter Geach (eds.), *Translations from the Philosophical Writings of Gottlob Frege*, 3rd edition (Oxford: Oxford University Press, 1980). See also Gottlob Frege, "The Thought" (translated by A. Quinton and M. Quinton), *Mind* 65 (1956), 289–311.

4. Paul Horwich, *Truth* (Oxford: Blackwell, 1990), p. 36. There is a slightly different account of what is involved in possessing the concept of truth in the second edition of the book. See *Truth*, 2nd edition (Oxford: Blackwell, 1998), p. 35.

5. Deflationism implies that one can use the concept of truth without fear of adverse *philosophical* or *empirical* consequences, but it does not imply that the concept is altogether innocuous. Thus, as far as I know, there is no version of deflationism in the literature that provides relief from the Liar Paradox. To provide relief from the Liar, in the sense intended here, it would be necessary to show that the intuitions about truth which contribute to the derivation of contradictions are somehow delusive, and can therefore be explained away. No deflationist has done this. Moreover, as I attempt to show in Chapter 6, it would be a mistake to try.

6. A. J. Ayer, *Language, Truth and Logic* (London: Gollancz, 1936); Dorothy Grover, Joseph L. Camp. Jr, and Nuel Belnap, "A Prosentential Theory of Truth," *Philosophical Studies* 27 (1975), 73–125; Hartry Field, "Deflationist Views of Meaning and Content," *Mind* 103 (1994), 249–85; Stephen Leeds, "Theories of Reference and Truth," *Erkenntnis* 13 (1978), 111–27; W. V. Quine, *Philosophy of Logic* (Englewood Cliffs, NJ: Prentice Hall, 1970); F. P. Ramsey, "Facts and Propositions," *Proceedings of the Aristotelian Society* supplementary volume 7 (1927), 153–70; P. F. Strawson, "Truth," *Proceedings of the Aristotelian Society* supplementary volume 24 (1950), 129–56. There is also a paper by the present writer that may be worth mentioning, viz., "Rudiments of a Theory of Reference," *Notre Dame Journal of Formal Logic* 28 (1987), 200–19. It explores several deflationary (or quasi-delationary) options that are not discussed in the forementioned works.

7. Translation by W. D. Ross, quoted from Richard McKeon (ed.), *The Basic Works of Aristotle* (New York: Random House, 1941), p. 749.

8. This is not a novel way of reading Aristotle. Thus, for example, Marian David describes the passage I've quoted as having "a rather deflationary flavor." See his *Correspondence and Disquotation* (Oxford: Oxford University Press, 1994), p. 18.

9. Plato might be said to be another precursor of Horwich, for his account of truth and falsity in the *Sophist* (at 240e and 263b) is virtually the same as Aristotle's.

10. Was Avicenna really the originator of the correspondence theory? For a brief but illuminating discussion of questions of priority, see Etienne Gilson, *History of Christian Philosophy in the Middle Ages* (New York: Random House, 1955), pp. 646–7 (note 26). Gilson quotes an early Latin translation of the relevant passage in Avicenna that runs as follows: "veritas . . . intelligitur dispositio dictionis vel intellectus qui significat dispositionem in re exteriore cum est ei aequalis." (I am indebted to Sandra Edwards and to Paul Vincent Spade for information about the influence of this passage in the Middle Ages.) Incidentally, while Gilson cites the passage as occurring at *Metaphysics* I, 4, Spade points out that it occurs in Chapter 8, not Chapter 4, of the standard Latin version of Avicenna's writings.

See S. Van Riet (ed.), *Avicenna Latinus: Liber de philosophia prima sive scientia divina*, vol. I (Louvain: E. Peeters, and Leiden: E. J. Brill, 1977). The passage occurs on p. 55.

11. *De Universo* I, 3, 26. See Guiliemi Alverni, *Omnia Opera*, vol. I (Orleans-Paris, 1674), p. 795. It may be that William deserves credit for originating the formulation that Aquinas made popular. Thus, his actual words are as follows: "intentio veritatis . . . ait Avicenna, est adaequatio orationis et rerum."

12. *Summa Theologica* I, q. 16, a. 2: "veritas est adaequatio rei et intellectus."

13. There are difficulties of interpretation which make it impossible to be sure about this. Thus, "res" was sometimes used by medieval philosophers with the significance of our word "fact." See, for example, Roy J. Deferrari, *A Latin-English Dictionary of St. Thomas Aquinas* (Boston: St. Paul Editions, 1986), p. 916.

14. Immanuel Kant, *Critique of Pure Reason*, translated by Norman Kemp Smith (New York: St. Martin's Press, 1965), p. 220 and p. 532.

15. Alfred Tarski, "The Concept of Truth in Formalized Languages," in Tarski's collection *Logic, Semantics, Metamathematics*, translated by J. H. Woodger (Oxford: Clarendon Press, 1956), pp. 152–278.

Unlike most contemporary writers who are concerned with truth, I will have very little to say about Tarski's theory. There are two reasons for this. One is that I am convinced that what I call objectualist versions of the correspondence theory are less well motivated than factualist versions. (This view is defended, albeit somewhat obliquely, in Chapter 3.) Second, I am concerned in this work with the project of explaining our grasp of the commonsense concept of propositional truth. It would only make sense to claim that our grasp of this notion admits of a Tarskian explanation if it could be shown that common sense is in possession of counterparts of the technical notions that provide the foundation for Tarski's theory of truth. In particular, this claim would only make sense if it could be shown that common sense is in possession of an extremely powerful counterpart of Tarski's notion of *satisfaction* – a counterpart that could be applied to the whole range of thoughts, regardless of logical structure. I feel sure that we are *not* in possession of such a notion. Indeed, even today, seventy years after the publication of Tarski's paper, the only available concepts of satisfaction are limited in application to representational schemes with an extremely impoverished range of logical structures. (I expand on these observations a bit in the Appendix to Chapter 4. For a lucid discussion of satisfaction, and also of attempts to generalize Tarski's original definition, see Ken Taylor, *Truth and Meaning* [Oxford: Blackwell, 1998].)

As I see it, then, Tarski's theory of truth is poorly motivated, relative to the class of correspondence theories, and it has no bearing on the task of explaining our commonsense thought and talk about truth. There is, however, a dimension of Tarski's work that I applaud. Thus, as Hartry Field pointed out a number of years ago ("Tarski's Theory of Truth," *Journal of Philosophy* LXIX [1972], 347–75), while Tarski's theory of truth can be seen as a form of the correspondence theory, his understanding of our *relational* semantic concepts (e.g., reference, denotation) appears to have been fully deflationary in character. Accordingly, there is a significant overlap between Tarski's views and the views that I will be developing.

16. Bertrand Russell, *The Problems of Philosophy* (Oxford: Oxford University Press, 1912), p. 129.

17. See Ludwig Wittgenstein, *Tractatus Logico-Philosophicus*, translated by D. F. Pears and B. F. McGuiness (London: Routledge and Kegan Paul, 1961), especially 2.21, 4.022, 4.023, and 4.25; and G. E. Moore, *Some Main Problems of Philosophy* (London: George Allen and Unwin, 1953), p. 277. (I am indebted to my colleague Edward Minar for help in connection with understanding the cited passages in the *Tractatus*.)

18. J. L. Austin, "Truth," *Proceedings of the Aristotelian Society*, supplementary volume 24 (1950), 111–28.

19. See D. M. Armstrong, *A World of States of Affairs* (Cambridge: Cambridge University Press, 1997).

20. It is arguable that the English term "refers" is used to express two quite different concepts. Thus, consider the following sentences:

(★) The proposition that Achilles had a magnificent shield cannot be said to correspond to an extraconceptual state of affairs, because the concept of Achilles does not refer to anything.

($) The proposition that Achilles had a magnificent shield is about Achilles, because the concept of Achilles refers to Achilles.

It is tempting to suppose that (★) and ($) can both be used to make true claims. If this supposition is correct, there must be two concepts of reference, for it is impossible for both (★) and ($) to be true unless "refers" expresses a different concept in (★) than in ($).

Let us suppose that this argument is sound, and that there are in fact two concepts of reference corresponding respectively to (★) and to ($). We can say that these concepts are distinguished by the fact that the first one, and only the first one, is governed by the following inference pattern:

The concept of *a* refers to *b*.
_____

Therefore, there exists an actual entity to which the concept of *a* refers.

In other words, the first concept differs from the second in that it is existence-entailing with respect to its second argument place.

There are several reasons for thinking that the first of these two notions of reference is much more important than the second. (One such reason will emerge in Chapter 5, which argues that the former notion plays an essential role in a well confirmed empirical theory.) Accordingly, I will be concerned exclusively in the present work with the former notion.

CHAPTER 2. TRUTH IN THE REALM OF THOUGHTS

1. Paul Horwich, *Truth* (Oxford: Blackwell, 1990).

2. Saul A. Kripke, *Naming and Necessity* (Cambridge, MA: Harvard University Press, 1980).

3. The skepticism I describe here is not unrelated to the sort of skepticism that W. V. Quine defends in *Word and Object* (Cambridge, MA: MIT Press,1960), chapter II.

There are, however, enormous differences, the most important of which is that the skepticism to which I refer is skepticism about the semantic properties of concepts and thoughts, while Quinean skepticism is skepticism about the semantic properties of words and sentences.

It is worth adding, perhaps, that despite being concerned with a different issue, my remarks in the text concerning the untenability of semantic skepticism about concepts appear to have important (negative) implications concerning Quinean skepticism about the denotations of words. As is well known, Quine maintains that it is factually indeterminate whether "gavagai," a term in a certain jungle language, denotes rabbits – rather than, say, undetached rabbit parts. To see that this view is highly problematic, observe first that the following claim is quite plausible: "gavagai" denotes rabbits as used by speakers of the jungle language if (a) the speakers of the jungle language possess the concept of a rabbit, (b) the speakers in question use "gavagai" to express that concept, and (c) the concept of a rabbit denotes rabbits. Assuming that this is correct, and assuming also that skepticism about the denotation of the concept of a rabbit is absurd, we may conclude that Quine's skepticism about the denotation of "gavagai" stands or falls with the following two claims: (i) the question of whether the speakers of the jungle language possess the concept of a rabbit does not have a determinate answer; and (ii) the question of whether the speakers of the jungle language use "gavagai" to express a particular component of their conceptual lexicon does not have a determinate answer. That is to say, given that skepticism about the denotation of the concept of a rabbit is absurd, it seems that Quinean skepticism must be rejected unless (i) or (ii) is correct. But there are grounds for doubting both (i) and (ii). Thus, as will be urged at some length in Chapter 5, it seems that the question of whether an agent possesses a concept like the concept of a rabbit can be settled by appeal to facts about the agent's functional organization and facts about the agent's informational relations to the world. And, furthermore, it is quite plausible that the question of whether an agent uses "gavagai" to express a given concept can be settled by appeal to facts about the agent's functional organization.

4. See Anil Gupta, "Minimalism," *Philosophical Perspectives* 7 (1993), 359–69.
5. It is undeniable that we accept (11) and (12), but someone might object to the claim that we accept (10), citing in justification the fact that we are disposed to apply the word "true" to such nonthoughts as sentences, beliefs, and utterances. My response to this objection is that the word "true" is ambiguous. It is used to express a variety of concepts – one that applies to thoughts, one that applies to sentences, and so on. Because of this ambiguity, the fact that we are disposed to apply "true" to entities of different kinds is fully compatible with saying that we accept (10).

Why maintain that "true" is used to express several different concepts rather than a single concept that can be applied to a range of entities? There are several reasons. Here I will just remind the reader that we have intuitions to the effect that the concept of sentential truth depends upon – in the sense of being reductively explainable in terms of – the concept of propositional truth. Specifically, we have intuitions which strongly suggest that we are committed to the following definition: where $S$ is a sentence (of language $L$), $S$ is true (in $L$) if and only if there is a proposition $P$ such that (i) $S$ expresses $P$ (in $L$), and (ii) $P$ is true. It is clear that this definition presupposes that the concept of sentential truth is distinct from the concept of propositional truth.

6. The discussion in the text might suggest that the force of Gupta's reasoning is quite limited in scope, applying exclusively to (10) and to generalizations which, like (11) and (12), are concerned with the truth-conditional semantic properties of logical concepts. By the same token, it might therefore be thought possible to block the objection by the simple expedient of enriching minimalism a bit – that is, by simply adding (10) and propositions like (11) and (12) as new axioms. (The axioms would thus come to encompass instances of (T), (10), and propositions like (11) and (12).) In fact, however, it is possible to formulate Gupta's objection in terms of propositions that are altogether different in form and content from (10)–(12). Thus, for example, as Gupta points out, it is reasonable to suppose that a theory of truth should contribute to the explanation of generalizations that capture the relationships between the concept of truth and such other semantic concepts as the concepts of reference and denotation. Here is an example:

An atomic thought consisting of a predicate concept $F$ and a nominal concept $a$ is true if and only if $a$ refers to an object that is denoted by $F$.

Again, it is reasonable to suppose that a theory of truth should explain generalizations that are concerned with the truth or falsity of thoughts that are themselves concerned with truth or falsity. What I have in mind here are generalizations like this one:

For any $x$ and $y$, if $x$ is a thought that attributes truth to another thought $y$, then $x$ is true if $y$ is true.

There are still other categories of general propositions that a theory of truth should explain. It is clear, I think, that if we were to attempt to deal with all of these categories by simply adding their members to minimalism as new axioms, we could not claim to have thereby vindicated minimalism. Rather, we would have replaced minimalism with an entirely different theory – a theory, moreover, that is entirely lacking in such virtues as simplicity and systematic unity.

7. See, for example, Merrie Bergmann, James Moor, and Jack Nelson, *The Logic Book*, 3rd edition (New York: McGraw-Hill, 1998). It might also be useful to consult the Appendix to Chapter 6, where I argue that we are forced to adopt rules like the ones stated here by the very meanings of the quantifiers *some* and *all*.

8. In addition to substitutional quantifiers that bind propositional variables, there are also substitutional quantifiers that bind nominal variables – that is, variables that occupy positions in thoughts that can also be occupied by nominal concepts. Interestingly, in addition to its being possible to distinguish between substitutional quantifiers that bind propositional variables and the usual nonsubstitutional (or *objectual*) quantifiers, it is also possible to distinguish between substitutional quantifiers that bind nominal variables and objectual quantifiers. This is because, unlike objectual quantifiers, substitutional quantifiers can appropriately bind variables that occur in hyperintensional contexts (such as contexts of the form *believes*

*that p*). In order to accommodate this difference in the logical behavior of the two types of quantifier, it is necessary to state rules of inference for objectual quantifiers that are more restrictive than the corresponding rules for substitutional quantifiers. In particular, the introduction rules for the former quantifiers have to be restricted so as to prevent their being prefixed to hyperintensional contexts. It follows that there would be no risk of ambiguity if one were to define nominal substitutional quantifiers by formulating rules of inference.

9. Occasionally interlocutors have expressed a sense of discomfort concerning the expression "open thought," maintaining that there could not be such a thing as a thought that was not semantically determinate in every respect. If the reader shares this feeling, I request that he or she view "open thought" as a purely technical term, meaning something like "structure obtained from a thought by replacing one or more of its constituents with a propositional variable."

10. Simple substitutionalism is not the only theory that provides an answer to Gupta's criticism of Horwich's account of truth. An alternative is presented on p. 259 of Hartry Field's "Deflationist Views of Meaning and Content," *Mind* 103 (1994), 249–85. These two proposals are very closely related, however: As Field observes, his proposal makes use of a device that "corresponds to a very weak fragment of a substitutional quantificational language." Here is his formulation of the proposal: "One alternative is to incorporate schematic letters for sentences into the language, reasoning with them as variables; and then to employ two rules of inference governing them: (i) a rule that allows replacement of all instances of a schematic letter by a sentence; (ii) a rule that allows inference of $\forall x(\text{Sentence}(x) \supset A(x))$ from the schema $A("p")$, where $A("p")$ is a schema in which all occurrences of the schematic letter $p$ are surrounded by quotes."

Field's proposal is attractive, but I feel that there is a strong reason for preferring the approach to truth that is recommended in the text. Thus, as I see it, Field's proposal encounters grave difficulties when it is reformulated as a theory of the semantic concepts we apply to thoughts. (As the foregoing quotation attests, Field's idea was originally formulated as a proposal about truth predicates in natural languages.) Transposed to the arena of thoughts, it presupposes that it is possible to entertain propositional attitudes toward entities that are not thoughts but rather thought-schemas. (Specifically, it presupposes that we accept the thought-schema *the thought that p is true if and only if p*.) This appears to call for an abrupt departure from the way in which we normally think of propositional attitudes.

There is also a second problem with Field's view. Consider the following generalization:

It holds without exception that if the thought that things stand thus and so is true, then things really do stand thus and so.

I wish to make three claims about this generalization. First, we are disposed on reflection to accept it. Second, it is best understood as involving substitutional quantification. (A defense of this second claim is implicit in Section VII.) And third, there are many similar generalizations that we are disposed to accept. Putting these claims together, we arrive at the conclusion that we are disposed to accept a large class of propositions that link substitutional quantification to the concept of truth.

Assuming that this conclusion is correct, if a theory of truth is to explain all of our dispositions containing the concept of truth, it must credit us with possession of substitutional quantifiers. But Field's theory does not do this. Instead of crediting us with possession of substitutional quantifiers, it claims that we make essential use of unquantified schemas in reasoning about truth. It follows that Field's theory fails to discharge all of its explanatory obligations.

11. It is desirable to give explicit, quantifier-based definitions of reference and other semantic properties of concepts (instead of simply relying on instances of schemata like (R) and (D)) for the same reason that it is desirable to give explicit, quantifier-based definitions of truth and semantic correspondence. As Gupta points out, there are a priori generalizations involving reference and related concepts that cannot be explained by definitions based on (R) and (D).

12. The main idea of substitutionalism is that definitions of semantic concepts should make use of substitutional quantifiers. A number of authors have formulated this idea as a claim about the concepts that we use in thinking about the semantic properties of linguistic expressions; see, for example, the discussion in Marian David, *Correspondence and Disquotation* (Oxford: Oxford University Press, 1993). As far as I know, the present work is the only place in which the idea takes the form of a claim about the concepts that we use in thinking about the semantic properties of thoughts.

13. W. V. Quine, *Philosophy of Logic* (Englewood Cliffs, NJ: Prentice Hall, 1970).

14. Stephen Leeds, "Theories of Reference and Truth," *Erkenntnis* 13 (1978), 111–29.

15. To elaborate: Substitutional quantifiers make it possible for one to endorse or affirm a thought without explicitly entertaining that thought and without describing its content. We see this feature, for example, in $(\Sigma p)((\textit{Fermat's Last Theorem} = \textit{the thought that } p) \textit{ and } p)$. To embrace this proposition is to commit oneself to the content of Fermat's Last Theorem, but the proposition gives no indication of what that content might be. In general, instances of the open thought $(\Sigma p)((x = \textit{the thought that } p) \textit{ and } p)$ enable one to endorse target thoughts even though in entertaining the instances one is entertaining thoughts *about* the target thoughts rather than the target thoughts themselves.

It is clear, then, that substitutional quantification enables the expression of indefinite endorsements, and that it is therefore capable of serving one of the purposes that Quine attributes to the concept of truth. But Quine also claims that truth enables the expression of *generalized* endorsements. Is this true of substitutional quantification as well? Yes. In fact, substitutional quantification contributes to the expression of generality in two ways. First, of course, when the quantifier $(\Pi p)$ occurs in a proposition like $(\Pi p)$ *(if Jones believes that p, then p)*, it is being used to make a generalized endorsement. Second, the construction $(\Sigma p)((x = \textit{the thought that } p) \textit{ and } p)$ contributes to the expression of generality in a rather different way. In addition to making it possible for one to endorse particular thoughts while identifying those thoughts only by name or by content-neutral description (as in $(\Sigma p)((\textit{Fermat's Last Theorem} = \textit{the thought that } p) \textit{ and } p)$), the construction $(\Sigma p)((x = \textit{the thought that } p) \textit{ and } p)$ makes it possible for one to commit oneself to all of the members of a *set* of thoughts without explicitly entertaining the thoughts and without appealing in any way to their contents. Thus, combining the open thought *($\Sigma p$)((x = the thought that p) and p)* with an *objectual* universal quantifier that ranges over thoughts, it is possible to frame thoughts like *(x)(if Jones believes x, then ($\Sigma p$)((x = the thought that p) and p))*. It is clear that such thoughts are equivalent to generalized endorsements involving the quantifier *($\Pi p$)*.

In view of these considerations, it is clear that substitutional quantifiers are ideally suited to play a role in thought and discourse that is strongly equivalent to the role that Quine claims for the concept of truth.

16. See, for example, Dorothy Grover, Joseph L. Camp, Jr. and Nuel Belnap, "A Prosentential Theory of Truth," *Philosophical Studies* 27 (1975), 73–125.

17. Ludwig Wittgenstein, *Philosophical Investigations*, 3rd edition (New York: Macmillan, 1958), pp. 51–2.

18. See A. N. Prior, *Objects of Thought* (Oxford: Oxford University Press, 1971); and "Correspondence Theory of Truth," in Paul Edwards (ed.), *The Encyclopedia of Philosophy*, vol. 2 (New York: Macmillan, 1967), pp. 223–32. See also Dorothy Grover, *A Prosentential Theory of Truth* (Princeton, NJ: Princeton University Press, 1992). The following chapters are especially relevant: Chapter 5, "Prosentences and Quantification: A Response to Zimmerman," pp. 137–45, and Chapter 6, "Truth," pp. 146–72.

There is a significant difference of detail between the claims of these authors and the views recommended in the text: neither Prior nor Grover cites the expression "so-and-so" as a propositional variable or prosentence. Nor does any other philosopher with whom I am acquainted. It sometimes happens, though, that philosophers *use* "so-and-so" as a prosentence. Here is an example: "An element *E represents* that so-and-so, or it is the case that so-and-so according to *E*, iff, necessarily, if *E* is selected, then so-and-so." This passage is quoted from David Lewis, *On the Plurality of Worlds* (Oxford: Basil Blackwell, 1996), p. 175.

19. See Saul A. Kripke, *Naming and Necessity* (Cambridge, MA: Harvard University Press, 1980); and Hilary Putnam, "The Meaning of 'Meaning,'" in Putnam's collection of essays, *Mind, Language, and Reality* (Cambridge: Cambridge University Press, 1975), pp. 215–71.

20. Kripke, *op. cit.*, p. 91.

21. See Jerry A. Fodor, *Psychosemantics* (Cambridge, MA: MIT Press, 1987); and *A Theory of Content and Other Essays* (Cambridge, MA: MIT Press, 1990). Michael Devitt was one of the earliest defenders of this view. See his *Designation* (New York: Columbia University Press, 1981).

22. In saying that (S) might correspond only very roughly to structures that are actually present in the mind, I am in effect acknowledging that it might be necessary to replace simple substitutionalism with a somewhat different substitutional theory in order to attain full descriptive adequacy. What might such an alternative substitutional theory look like?

I will mention two possibilities.

First, there is the theory that our concept of truth is defined by the following pair of propositions:

($) ($\Pi p$)(the thought that p is true if and only if p).
(%) For any x, if x is true, then ($\Sigma p$)(x = the thought that p).

(S) is deducible from ($) and (%), and there are also proofs running from (S) to ($) and to (%). (A qualification: the proof running from (S) to ($) requires an additional premise – viz., *(Πp)(Πq)(if the thought that p = the thought that q, then p if and only if q).*) Thus, the relationship between simple substitutionalism and the theory consisting of ($) and (%) is quite intimate. But there is a significant difference in explanatory power. To see this, observe that it is much easier to derive the instances of schema (T) from ($) than to derive them from (S). Because of this fact, the present theory is in a much better position than simple substitutionalism to explain why the instances of (T) strike us as trivial.

Second, there is the theory which claims, first, that our concept of truth is defined by ($) and (%), and second, that the mind is equipped with the following rule of inference:

*Quantifier Conversion (QC)*

(Π**p**)(... the thought that **p** ...)
_____

For any thought **x** (. . . **x** . . .)

This theory does not claim that QC contributes directly to the content of the concept of truth. Rather, it appeals to QC in explaining how the mind is able to arrive at general beliefs like (11) and (12).

In general, explanations that appeal to QC are simpler than explanations that do not. To see this, suppose that an agent has proved the following thought:

(★) (Πp)(Πq)(Πr)(If the thought that p = the thought that if q then r, and it is the case that p and also the case that q, then it is the case that r as well.)

(The proof requires only the principle *(Πp)(Πq)(if the thought that p = the thought that q, then p if and only if q)*, standard deductive reasoning, and three applications of the introduction rule for the universal substitutional quantifier.) It is not difficult to see that, in the presence of QC, it is possible to move from (★) to (★★):

(★★) For any thoughts x, y, and z, if x = the conditional consisting of y and z, in that order, and it is the case that x is true and also the case that y is true, then it is the case that z is true as well.

(The derivation has three premises – (★), ($), and the principle *(Πp)(Πq)(Πr)((the thought that p = the thought that if q then r) if and only if (the thought that p = the conditional consisting of the thought that q and the thought that r, in that order))*. It involves three applications of QC.) As this example shows, if a theory represents the mind as equipped with QC, it is able to explain why the mind is able to apprehend the truth of generalizations like (★★) quickly and effortlessly.

There is an illuminating discussion of rules like QC in Daniel Isaacson, "Some Considerations on Arithmetical Truth and the ω Rule," in Michael Detlefsen (ed.), *Proof, Logic and Formalization* (London: Routledge, 1992), pp. 94–138.

I will continue in the text to use simple substitutionalism as my primary example of a substitutional theory of truth. It is, after all, extremely simple and extremely elegant. As the present examples show, however, the structures postulated by an alternative substitutional theory might well turn out to have a higher degree of psychological reality than (S).

CHAPTER 3. THE MARRIAGE OF HEAVEN AND HELL

1. See Donald Davidson, *Essays on Actions and Events* (Oxford: Clarendon Press, 1980).

2. There are several comprehensive and penetrating appraisals of Davidson's arguments in the literature. Two of the best are Jonathan Bennett's *Events and their Names* (Indianapolis: Hackett, 1988) and Hugh Mellor's *The Facts of Causation* (London: Routledge, 1995). These authors wind up with conclusions that cohere nicely with the position about Davidson's views that is adopted in the text. For a quite different take on the issues, see the editors' introduction and James Higginbotham's contribution to J. Higginbotham, F. Pianesi, and A. Varzi (eds.), *Speaking of Events* (New York: Oxford, 2000).

3. It is, for example, quite plausible that certain types of perception-reports carry a commitment to states of affairs. See J. Barwise, "Scenes and Other Situations," *The Journal of Philosophy* 77 (1981), 369–97. There is a defense of Barwise's position in S. Neale, "Events and 'Logical Form,'" *Linguistics and Philosophy* 11 (1988), 303–21. For the other side of the story, see J. Higginbotham, "The Logic of Perceptual Reports: An Extensional Alternative to Situation Semantics," *Journal of Philosophy* 80 (1983), 100–27.

4. The view that our commitment to states of affairs is grounded in our perceptions concerning the structure of the world is familiar from Wittgenstein's *Tractatus* and the secondary literature that is concerned with that work. Here, for example, is George Pitcher's formulation of the view: "If you break the world down into objects, the result does not correspond uniquely to this actual world; any number of other possible, but non-actual worlds, if so broken down, would yield the same result. . . . It is the facts that there are, not the objects that there are, that uniquely determine the world – i.e., this actual world, as distinguished from other possible worlds." *The Philosophy of Wittgenstein* (Englewood Cliffs, NJ: Prentice Hall, 1964).

5. Descriptions of the form *the state of affairs x such that, necessarily, x is actual if and only if p* presuppose a doctrine about actuality that can be expressed as follows:

(D) For every possible world *w*, a proposition of the form *the state of affairs that p is actual* has the same truth value at *w* as the corresponding proposition of the form *p*.

To see that (D) really is presupposed by descriptions of the given form, suppose that the proposition *the state of affairs that snow is white is actual* has a different truth value in some world than that the proposition *snow is white*. Under this assumption, it is a mistake to ascribe necessity to the following proposition: *the state of affairs that snow is white is actual if and only if snow is white*. But then the description *the state of affairs x such that necessarily, x is actual if and only if snow is white* fails to have the referent that we want it to have – the state of affairs that snow is white.

137

(D) is supported by vivid intuitions. Thus, for example, we have intuitions to the effect that if snow is green in a certain possible world, then that world shows that the state of affairs that snow is green could have been actual. These intuitions appear to commit us to saying that if the proposition *snow is green* is true in a world *w*, then the proposition *the state of affairs that snow is green is actual* is true in *w*, too.

It must be acknowledged, however, there is also intuitive support for the following opposing doctrine:

(D′) For every possible world *w*, a proposition of the form *the state of affairs that p is actual* is true at *w* just in case the corresponding proposition of the form *p* is true at *this* world, that is, the world in which the reader and I live and move and have our being.

To appreciate the merits of (D′), consider the following proposition: *if I had been wiser in my stock purchases, then many pleasant states of affairs would now obtain that do not actually obtain*. The antecedent of this conditional invites us to consider a certain possible world *w*, and the consequent gives us a proposition that purports to be true in *w* – the proposition *many pleasing states of affairs obtain that do not actually obtain*. It is clear, however, that the question of whether the consequent is true in *w* does not depend entirely on the states of affairs that obtain in *w*. To determine whether the consequent is true in *w*, we must compare the states of affairs that obtain in *w* to the states of affairs that obtain in *this* world, asking whether some of the pleasant members of the former class fail to belong to the latter class. Furthermore, it is clear that it is the constituent *actually* that thus directs our attention away from *w* and towards this world. *Actually* here refers to this world, despite the fact that it occurs in a proposition that is primarily concerned with a different world.

The tension we are observing here is not limited to intuitions about propositions that attribute actuality to states of affairs. Similar tensions arise in connection with all propositions about actuality – for example, propositions that attribute actuality to individual substances. These tensions have long been familiar to metaphysicians and logicians. Thus, David Lewis has called attention to the following examples:

(1) The following is contingent: in the actual world, Caesar is murdered.
(2) There could have been objects other than those there actually are.

As Lewis points out, we seem to regard both of these propositions as true; but (1) presupposes that the reference of *actual* can shift from world to world, while (2) presupposes that *actual* refers rigidly to this world. (See Lewis, *Philosophical Papers*, vol. I (New York: Oxford University Press, 1983), p. 22. Lewis adapts (1) from a paper by Peter van Inwagen, and borrows (2) from a note by Allen Hazen. See van Inwagen, "Indexicality and Actuality," *The Philosophical Review* LXXXIX (1980), 403–26; and Hazen, "One of the Truths about Actuality," *Analysis* 39 (1979), 1–3.)

The most natural way to solve the problem posed by these conflicts is, it seems, to suppose that we have two concepts of actuality, one that conforms to the principle that the question of whether a proposition about actuality is true at a possible world *w* depends on how things stand in *w*, and another that conforms to the principle that the question of whether a proposition about actuality is true at a possible world $w$ depends on how things stand in this world. This is, at all events, the view that I will adopt here. On this view, we possess a concept that satisfies (D), and therefore, we possess a concept that fulfills the presuppositions of descriptions of the form *the state of affairs x such that, necessarily, x is actual if and only if p.*

6. My suggestion here about the nature of correspondence is similar in some respects to one that is sketched by Paul Horwich in section 36 of *Truth* (Oxford: Blackwell, 1990). However, the concept of correspondence that I define has a much more inclusive range of application than the one that Horwich defines. (The concept that I define can be applied to all propositions, regardless of logical structure. On the other hand, it appears that Horwich's concept can be applied only to atomic propositions – that is, to propositions built out of relational concepts and sets of individual concepts.)

7. Perhaps it will be useful to state briefly what I take to be the logical and semantic properties of canonical names of the form *the thought that p.*

As I see it, *the thought that* is an operator that can combine with thoughts to produce names of thoughts – specifically, an operator that can combine with any thought $T$ to produce a concept that functions as a name of $T$. Thus, thoughts of the form *the thought that p* can be said to *display* the very thoughts that they serve to name.

It follows from this view that the operator *the thought that* is closely analogous to quotation marks, for quotation marks can combine with any sentence $S$ to produce a name of $S$. By the same token, quotation marks can be said to display the very sentences that they serve to name.

8. Earlier versions of Section V have occasionally elicited the objection that the analysis of semantic correspondence that is offered in that section is circular. The rationale that has been given for this charge can be summarized as follows: "Since (SC) claims to offer an analysis of the concept of semantic correspondence, it is circular if it contains a concept that signifies the relation of correspondence. But (SC) does contain such a concept – the operator *the state of affairs that.* This operator attaches to thought contents to yield names of states of affairs. Accordingly, it signifies a function that maps thought contents onto states of affairs. Reflection shows that this function must be the very relation that (SC) purports to explain."

To see that this rationale is badly flawed, recall the theory of meaning for canonical names that is recommended in Section IV. That theory claims that names of the form *the state of affairs that p* are equivalent in content to descriptions of the form *the state of affairs x such that, necessarily, x is actual if and only if p.* No such description has a function from thought contents to states of affairs as its semantic value. Moreover, inspection shows that the semantic values of the constituents of such descriptions can be fully specified without mentioning a function of the given sort.

9. It seems incontestable that the instances of (A) are *true*; they are endorsed by compelling intuitions. But also, in addition to finding them true, I suspect that the reader will be strongly inclined to share my view that they are a priori and necessary. (I do not wish to say that all propositions of the given form are necessary – regardless of which concept of actuality they contain. On the contrary,

139

In footnote 5, a distinction is drawn between two concepts of actuality – one which conforms to the principle that whether a proposition about actuality is true at a possible world $w$ depends on how things stand in $w$, and another which conforms to the principle that whether a proposition about actuality is true at $w$ depends on how things stand in *this* world. Only those propositions of form (A) that contain the first of these concepts are necessary (unless the states of affairs to which they attribute actuality are necessary in their own right).)

In fact, it is possible to construct a *proof* to the effect that instances of (A) are a priori and necessary – or, at least, it is possible to construct such a proof if the theory of meaning for canonical names of states of affairs that is given in Section IV is correct. To see this, observe that when we apply that theory to an instance of (A), we find that the instance is equivalent to a proposition of the following form:

$(\exists x)(x$ is a state of affairs & $\Box(x$ is actual $\leftrightarrow p)$ & $(\forall y)(\Box(y$ is actual $\leftrightarrow p) \rightarrow y = x)) \rightarrow [(\exists x)(x$ is a state of affairs & $\Box(x$ is actual $\leftrightarrow p)$ & $(\forall y)(\Box(y$ is actual $\leftrightarrow p) \rightarrow y = x)$ & $x$ is actual$) \leftrightarrow p]$.

Instances of this schema can be shown to be logically true by using standard deductive techniques. But of course, logically true propositions are a priori and necessary. (Here I am presupposing the standard theory of descriptions. See, e.g., Merrie Bergmann, James Moor, and Jack Nelson, *The Logic Book*, 3rd edition (New York: McGraw-Hill, 1998), section 7.9.)

10. What I have said about actuality in this section can also be said, *mutatis mutandis*, about the concepts of obtaining and realization. Thus, it appears that the following counterparts of (A$\star$) are both true:

(O$\star$) ($\Pi p$)(if the state of affairs that $p$ exists, then the state of affairs that $p$ obtains if and only if $p$).

(R$\star$) ($\Pi p$)(if the state of affairs that $p$ exists, then the state of affairs that $p$ is realized if and only if $p$).

Further, (O$\star$) and (R$\star$) combine with (T$\star$) to generate counterparts of (AT$\star$):

(OT$\star$) ($\Pi p$)(if the state of affairs that $p$ exists, then the thought that $p$ is true if and only if the state of affairs that $p$ obtains).

(RT$\star$) ($\Pi p$)(if the state of affairs that $p$ exists, then the thought that $p$ is true if and only if the state of affairs that $p$ is realized).

It follows that (A$\star$) is not the only source of truthmaker intuitions – that is, of intuitions to the effect that whether a thought is true depends on how things are arranged in the world.

11. It may strike the reader that a fanatical substitutionalist like myself should hasten to embrace the *substitutional theory of actuality* – that is, the theory that the concept of actuality can be analyzed as follows:

For any state of affairs $x$, $x$ is actual if and only if ($\Sigma p$)(($x =$ the state of affairs that $p$) and $p$).

This theory is at first sight extremely tempting, for in addition to having plausible consequences (viz., the instances of schema (A)), it enjoys great simplicity and elegance. There are, however, several considerations that count strongly against it. I will mention three.

First, as we saw in footnote 5, it is plausible that there are two very different concepts of actuality. It is clearly impossible to give a single analysis of both of these concepts. Thus, the substitutional theory cannot be said to tell the whole truth about actuality. (At most it succeeds in explaining the first of the two concepts.)

Second, if the analysis of canonical names for states of affairs that is given in Section IV is correct, then the substitutional theory of actuality is circular. According to that analysis, concepts of the form *the state of affairs that p* abbreviate complex descriptions that contain the concept of actuality. Thus, if that analysis is correct, it would be circular to make use of concepts of the given form in explaining actuality.

Third, there is a problem with the substitutional theory that can be formulated as follows: "The substitutional theory offers an explanation of what it is for a certain class of states of affairs to be actual – specifically, all and only those states of affairs picked out by canonical names of the form *the state of affairs that p*. But it appears that there are a great many states of affairs that are not picked out by such names. Thus, in its proper deployment, "thought" appears to apply only to representational states of finite complexity. ("Thought" derives from folk psychology, and folk psychology appears to be concerned only with the mental states of finite beings.) But it is reasonably clear that there are many states of affairs that cannot be captured by finitary representations. It follows that there are many states of affairs that do not have canonical names, including presumably many states of affairs that count as actual. This spells trouble for the substitutional theory."

Someone might respond to this argument by saying that, whatever may be the case with the conception of thoughts that is built into folk psychology, it is possible to extend that conception along the lines suggested by the modern theory of infinitary languages. (See, for example, Jon Barwise, "Infinitary Logics," in Evandro Agazzi (ed.), *Modern Logic: A Survey* (Dordrecht: D. Reidel, 1981), pp. 93–112.) This response seems correct as far as it goes, but I do not see that it is relevant. The question before us is one about the content of the commonsense notion of actuality. A conceptual analysis of that notion should make use only of the resources of our commonsense conceptual scheme.

12. Actually, the argument displayed in the text is an enthymeme. In order to derive (T$\star$) from (S) it is necessary to use the following additional assumption:

$$(\Pi p)(\Pi q)(\text{if the thought that } p = \text{the thought that } q, \text{ then } p \text{ if and only if } q).$$

Accordingly, this principle must be added to (SC), (S), and (A$\star$) in order to have an argument leading to (CP) that is deductively valid.

13. See Ernest W. Adams, *The Logic of Conditionals* (Dordrecht: D. Reidel, 1975). There is an attempt to sharpen Adams's argument in Ian Carlstrom and Christopher S. Hill, "Review of Adams's *The Logic of Conditionals*," *Philosophy of Science* 45 (1978), 155–8.

1. Like most philosophers, I owe my appreciation of the theoretical importance of determinate representations to the writings of Gareth Evans and John McDowell. Evans argued for the object dependence or "world involvingness" of indexical thoughts and concepts in *The Varieties of Reference* (Oxford: Clarendon Press, 1982). This idea is elaborated in McDowell's writings, most notably in the set of papers collected to form part II of *Meaning, Knowledge, and Reality* (Cambridge, MA: Harvard University Press, 1998).

2. I hasten to acknowledge, however, that definitions like (⋆) contain notions that are badly in need of clarification and defense. Unfortunately, it is impossible to address these issues without becoming rather deeply involved in complex questions about possession conditions for indexical concepts, and in particular, questions about the relationship between possession conditions for determinable indexical concepts and possession conditions for determinate indexical concepts. These questions lie beyond the scope of the present chapter, though I hope to return to them on another occasion.

3. Paul Horwich, *Truth* (Oxford: Blackwell, 1990).

4. See Horwich, ibid., p. 36: "A person's understanding of the truth predicate, 'is true' – his knowledge of its meaning – consists in his disposition to accept, without evidence, any instantiation of this schema,

   (E) 'The proposition that $p$ is true if and only if $p'$,

   by a declarative sentence of English (including any extension of English)." This account of the possession condition for truth is modified in the second edition of Horwich's book (Oxford: Blackwell, 1998), but the underlying idea remains pretty much the same.

5. This is intended to answer the "ideology objection" to Horwichian minimalism that Anil Gupta raises in "Minimalism," *Philosophical Perspectives* 7 (1993), 359–69 and "A Critique of Deflationism," *Philosophical Topics* 21 (1993), 57–81.

6. It might be useful to restate the argument of the last several paragraphs in somewhat different terms.

   I have maintained that if all of the clauses of a definition have a common form, then it is possible to reduce questions about mastery of the definition to questions about what is involved in possessing a cognitive grasp of a form – or in other words, to questions about what is involved in possessing a recognitional ability that is targeted on a form. I have also maintained, in effect, that our practice of attributing recognitional abilities to agents shows that we allow an agent to count as having a recognitional ability that is targeted on a form even if there are instances of the form that agent is unable to process due to the limitations of his or her cognitive capacities. It is sufficient that when the agent exercises the ability by making a recognitional judgment, it is the form itself (i.e., the relevant formal properties of things that have the form) that is causally responsible for the judgment. (This is a somewhat different way of putting the point about the induction schema and related formal objects.)

It seems that these claims are entirely correct, and that they decisively answer the objection under consideration – namely, the objection that AHM's explanation of the content of the concept of truth fails to cohere with its possession condition for that concept.

7. It is probably necessary to supplement (b) and (c) with a condition that will block Gettier counterexamples, but I do not know how to formulate such a condition.

8. It is not necessary for my purposes here to offer a detailed characterization of the principles that underlie Jones's translational abilities. It is enough to make a case for the claim that such abilities exist. But linguists have done some interesting work on the nature of certain related principles, identifying, for example, a transformation that changes the tenses of verbs in first order discourse (e.g., "My mind is on fire") into tenses that are appropriate for second order reports of such discourse ("He said that his mind was on fire"). See, for example, the discussions of "backshifting" in Randolph Quirk et al., *A Comprehensive Grammar of the English Language* (London: Longman, 1985).

9. For discussion of this point, see John Perry's classic essay, "The Essential Indexical," *Noûs* 13 (1979), 3–21.

10. See Donald Davidson, *Inquiries into Truth and Interpretation* (Oxford: Clarendon Press, 1984), pp. 17–36.

11. See, for example, Scott Soames, *Understanding Truth* (Oxford: Oxford University Press, 1999), chapter 3. (Soames uses locutions of the form "sentence $x$ is true relative to a sequence $s$" in place of more properly Tarskian locutions of the form "sentence $x$ is satisfied by sequence $s$.") There is another good account in Kenneth Taylor, *Truth and Meaning* (Oxford: Blackwell, 1998), chapter 3.


CHAPTER 5. WHY MEANING MATTERS

1. See, for example, John Pollock, *Contemporary Theories of Knowledge* (Savage, MD: Rowman and Littlefield, 1986), p. 165. See also Hartry Field, "Tarski's Theory of Truth," *The Journal of Philosophy* XLIX (1972), pp. 347–75; there is a discussion of the functions of truth in section V of this paper.

2. For further discussion, see Nelson Goodman's celebrated essay "About," which is included in his collection *Problems and Projects* (Indianapolis, MD: Bobbs-Merrill, 1972).

3. Christopher Peacocke, *A Study of Concepts* (Cambridge, MA: MIT Press, 1992). See also Peacocke, *Thoughts: A Study of Content* (Oxford: Blackwell, 1986).

4. Peacocke, *A Study of Concepts*, p. 6.

5. Peacocke, *A Study of Concepts*, pp. 7–8.

6. Here I am using italicization as a form of quasi-quotation.

7. See Gareth Evans, "Identity and Predication," *The Journal of Philosophy* LXXII (1975), 343–63.

8. When it is explained in terms of dispositions like the ones cited above, is it reasonable to say that the notion of an individuative judgment is nonsemantic in character? I think so. Thus, it is presumably possible to formulate possession conditions for color concepts like *white* without making essential use of semantic

notions, and the same is true of the concept of identity. (On the latter question, see Christopher S. Hill, "gavagai," *Analysis* XXXII (1972), 68–75.) Furthermore, although no one has yet shown how to do so in a satisfactory way, it is plausible that the notion of perceptual information about the environment can be explained in nonsemantic terms.

9. There is also a range of a priori principles that are concerned with *defeaters* of perceptual beliefs. Here is an example:

   Let $C$ be a natural kind concept that expresses a property $\phi$, and let $\phi$ be a natural kind that is observationally accessible. Given these assumptions, if $x$ is an agent who possesses $C$, then it must be the case that $x$ satisfies the following condition: If $x$ believes that the current external conditions of perception are such as to impede or distort the flow of information from external objects, or that his/her perceptual apparatus is not functioning properly, then, even if $x$'s current sensory state is such as to make it likely that a (sample of) $\phi$ is at hand, $x$ will not accept a recognitional judgment involving $C$.

   As I see it, possession conditions tend to be extremely complex, and this complexity is reflected in the family of general principles that captures their collective content.

10. The notion of probability that figures in principle (16) is meant to be a notion of probability that qualifies as more or less "objective" in character. If the reader is made uncomfortable by talk of *robustly* objective probabilities of nonrepeatable states of affairs, then he or she should construe my claims about probabilities as concerned with quantities induced via the relation of semantic correspondence from the subjective probabilities of an "ideal observer" – that is, from the subjective probabilities of an agent who satisfies certain idealized requirements concerning rationality and access to information.

11. See footnote 10.

12. I do not wish to claim that the value of our relational semantic notions can be exhaustively explained in terms of the uses of these notions that are discussed in the present chapter. Rather, I wish to claim only (a) that the uses that are described here are sufficient to show that the notions have considerable utility, and (b) that the uses in question are representative, and therefore provide a satisfactory basis for the conclusion that it is possible to combine substitutional analyses of the notions coherently with a full appreciation of their value.

    A more comprehensive account of the various uses of the notions would include a discussion of the fact that they are implicitly involved in our talk about the semantic properties of words and sentences. As we saw in Chapter 1, it appears that the semantic notions we use in connection with words and sentences are reducible to the notions we use in connection with concepts and thoughts. It follows from this that the semantic notions we use in connection with concepts and thoughts are implicitly involved in all of the practices in which the notions we use in connection with words and sentences play a role. And, by the same token, it follows that it is impossible to tell the full story of the value of the former notions without telling the story of the value of the latter notions.

    To illustrate: The notion of reference that we use in connection with words is useful because it enables us to state sociolinguistic generalizations like this one:

For any word $w$ and any place $p$, if $w$ refers to $p$ in language $L$, then it is possible for a group of speakers of $L$ to use $w$ to arrange to meet one another at $p$.

Assuming that the view recommended in Chapter 1 is correct, the notion of reference that we use in connection with concepts is implicitly involved in generalizations of this sort. (For further examples of the sort in question, see my "Rudiments of a Theory of Reference," *Notre Dame Journal of Formal Logic* 28 (1987), 200–19.)

13. Perhaps it will be useful to give another example. As we saw in Section II, relational semantic notions provide us with the means of generating a system of categories that can be used in restricting reliability-generalizations to various subject matters. Thus, for example, the notion of reference enables us to frame the following generalization:

($\star$) All of Warren's beliefs involving concepts that refer to cases of the decision problem are correct.

Does substitutional quantification make a similar contribution to the expressive power of our conceptual scheme? Yes. Thus, ($\star$) is equivalent to ($\$$):

($\$$) $(\forall x)$(if Warren believes $x$ and $(\Sigma a)(x$ involves the concept of $a$ and $a$ is a case of the decision problem), then $x$ is correct).

CHAPTER 6. INTO THE WILD BLUE YONDER

1. A. J. Ayer, *Language, Truth and Logic*, 2nd edition (London: Gollancz, 1946), p. 107.
2. According to the suggestion in the text, when we say that certain thoughts are neither true nor false, we are not to be taken literally. What we mean can be more accurately expressed by saying that the thoughts in question lack robust truth conditions – that is, by saying that they fail to correspond semantically to extraconceptual states of affairs.
   There is a second possibility. It may be that we have two concepts of truth, one that is defined by (S) and another that is defined in terms of the notion of robust truth conditions in the following way:

(#) For any $x$, $x$ is true if and only if there is a $y$ such that (a) $y$ is a state of affairs, (b) $y$ corresponds semantically to $x$, and (c) $y$ is actual.

Furthermore, it may be that we have a concept of falsity that has the following parallel definition:

(%) For any $x$, $x$ is false if and only if there is a $y$ such that (a) $y$ is a state of affairs, (b) $y$ corresponds semantically to $x$, and (c) $y$ fails to be actual.

Of course, if it is true that we have concepts of truth and falsity that are captured by these definitions, then our denials of bivalence can be taken literally. When we say, for example, that thoughts involving the concept of Achilles are neither true nor false, what we mean is that such thoughts fail to fit the requirements of (#) and (%).

This suggestion is a natural one, and it seems possible to me that it will turn out to be correct. (It would, of course, be a departure from the theory developed in earlier chapters to accept the view that there is a concept of truth that is captured by (#); but it would not be much of a departure, since that theory claims that we are in possession of all of the notions that figure in the definiens of (#).) There is, however, a reason for preferring the suggestion about denials of bivalence that is sketched in the text. The suggestion in the text counts as simpler than the present suggestion, for it credits us with only one concept of truth, while the present suggestion credits us with two.

Would it be possible to do away with the idea that we are in possession of a concept of truth that is governed by (S), maintaining that the concept that is governed by (#) is our sole concept of truth? No. For reasons that are given in the penultimate section of Chapter 3, and that are summarized briefly in the present section, it is indisputable that we are in possession of a concept of truth that is independent of the notion of robust truth conditions. It follows that any reasonable proposal that credits us with a concept that is governed by (#) must also credit us with another concept. And it follows from this in turn that any such proposal will be vulnerable to a simplicity objection.

Still, proposals of this sort have an appeal. For a sympathetic discussion of one such proposal (formulated, however, as a theory about our talk of *sentential* truth), see Brian McLaughlin and Vann McGee, "Distinctions Without a Difference," *Southern Journal of Philosophy* 33 (1995), 203–51.

3. Alfred Tarski, "The Concept of Truth in Formalized Languages," in J. H. Woodger (ed.), *Logic, Semantics, Metamathematics: Papers from 1923 to 1938* (Oxford: Clarendon Press, 1956), p. 267.

4. See, for example, Charles S. Chihara, "The Semantic Paradoxes: A Diagnostic Investigation," *Philosophical Review* 88 (1979), 590–618; and Charles S. Chihara, "The Semantic Paradoxes: Some Second Thoughts," *Philosophical Studies* 45 (1984), 223–9; and John L. Pollock, *How to Build a Person* (Cambridge, MA: MIT Press, 1989), pp. 158–60.

5. For what it is worth, my own favorites are Kripke's theory of fixed points and groundedness, and Gupta and Belnap's theory of circular definitions.

Kripke's approach to the Liar was originally presented in Saul A. Kripke, "Outline of a Theory of Truth," *Journal of Philosophy* 72 (1975), 690–716. There is an illuminating discussion of the theory in Scott Soames, *Understanding Truth* (Oxford: Oxford University Press, 1998), and a detailed and extremely clear explanation of how to apply Kripke's ideas to substitutional theories of truth in Vann McGee, "The Analysis of 'x is true' as 'For any p, if x = 'p', then p'," in André Chapuis and Anil Gupta (eds.), *Circularity, Definition, and Truth* (New Delhi: Indian Council of Philosophical Research, 2000), pp. 255–72. For an account of Gupta and Belnap's theory of the Liar, see Anil Gupta and Nuel Belnap, *The Revision Theory of Truth* (Cambridge, MA: MIT Press, 1993).

# Index

bivalence law (*cont.*)
    exceptions to, 114
    implied by substitutionalism, 112
    intuitions favoring, 114–15
    intuitions questioning, 109, 111–12, 114
Black, Max, 128n3

Camp, Joseph L., Jr., 5, 26, 128n6, 135n16
canonical names
    actuality-neutral concepts as, 46–48
    commitments concerning actuality of states of affairs, 46–48
    for concepts and thoughts, 48, 106, 139n7
    in semantic correspondence, 106
    thoughts and states of affairs related to, 48–9
Carlstrom, Ian, 141n13
causation
    Davidson's view of, 43–4
    internal connection between reference and, 29–30
causation, singular
    events as terms of, 43
    property-exemplifications as terms of, 42
Chapuis, Andre, 146n5
Chihara, Charles, 146n4
concepts
    as building blocks of propositions, 2
    eternal, 58, 60
    indexical, 10–11, 58, 63
    reference of, 29
    relational, 7, 91, 94, 106
    *See also* kind concepts
conjunction concept, 95
constructive dilemma principle, 125
correspondence intuitions

about truth, 39–40
    commitment to (CT), 54
    expressed by CP, 52–4
    state of affairs concept in, 41–6
correspondence theory of truth, 6, 39, 51
    advocates of, 6
    commitment to, 54–5
    factualist form of, 6
    intuitions favoring, 6–7, 51
    intuitions related to, 39–40
    objection to, 54–5
    objectualist form of, 6
    *See also* semantic correspondence

David, Marian, 128n8, 134n12
Davidson, Donald, 43, 86–7, 137n1, 143n10
Defarrari, Roy, 129n13
deflationary theory
    Horwich's minimalism [example], 4
    indexical representations as problems for, 58
deflationism
    appeal of, 4
    correspondence intuitions and, 38–41
    definition of, 3–4
    relationship to extended substitutionalism, 56–7
    *See also* substitutionalism, simple
denotation
    defined by propositions of form (D), 11
    definition of, 38
    as relational semantic concept, 7
Detlefsen, Michael, 136n22
Devitt, Michael, 135n21
disjunction
    constructive dilemma as natural elimination rule for, 125

148

Disjunction Introduction, 73
  modifying rules of, 126
  natural introduction rules for,
    125
  substitutional quantifier as
    generalized, 125
Disjunction Introduction, 73

eternal concept or thought, 58, 60
Evans, Gareth, 142n1, 143n7
events
  as separate from states of affairs, 43
  terms of singular causation as, 43
existence
  notion of, 51
Existential Elimination
  restrictions governing, 22
  as rule of inference for substitutional
    quantifiers, 19–20, 118, 125
Existential Introduction, 22
  of existential substitutional
    quantification, 83–5
  inaccessible thoughts and, 84–5
  as rule of inference for substitutional
    quantifiers, 19
expression
  a posteriori folk principles
    concerned with semantic, 102–3
  as relational semantic concept, 7,
    231

falsity
  Aristotle's explanation of, 5
  natural definition of, 112
  Plato's account of, 128n9
Field, Hartry, 5, 128n6, 129n15,
    133n10, 143n1
Fodor, Jerry, 29, 32, 135n21
folk psychology
  conception of thoughts in, 141n11

goals of, 101
principles about semantic relations,
    101
propositional attitudes in, 50
relational semantic concepts in, 91,
    94, 101–6
Frege, Gottlieb, 128n3

Geach, Peter, 128n3
generalizations
  about semantic properties, 12–13
  empirical, 13–14
  formulation of, 94
  a priori, universal, 16–17
Gilson, Etienne, 128n10
Goodman, Nelson, 143n2
grasping, direct and indirect, 75–6, 85–6
Grover, Dorothy, 5, 18, 26, 27, 128n6,
    135n16
Gupta, Anil, 16–17, 131n4, 134n11,
    142n5, 146n5

Hazen, Allen, 138n5
Higginbotham, J., 138n2,3
Hill, Christopher S., 141n13, 144n8,
    144n12
Horwich, Paul, 4, 5, 64–5, 128n4,
    130n1, 139n6, 142nn3,4
Horwichian minimalism
  arguments for, 12–16
  Aristotle's anticipation of, 5
  claim about truth conditions made
    by, 85
  concerned with eternal
    representations, 64–5
  definition of, 11
  example of deflationary theory, 4
  extension to accommodate
    indexicality, 82
  modifying, 67

149

negation concept, classical, 69
Nelson, Jack, 132n7, 140n9

PC. *See* possession condition
PC∗. *See* possession condition (PC*)
Peacocke, Christopher, 94–6, 143nn3,4,5
Perry, John, 143n9
Pianesi, F., 137n2
Pitcher, George, 137n4
Pollock, John, 143n1, 146n4
possession condition, 94–6
  augmenting Horwichian minimalism
    with, 67
  for a concept, 94–6
  for concept of conjunction, 95
  for concept of truth, 65–6, 71
  for concept *red,* 95–6
  dependence on material or natural
    relations, 96–7
  for Existential Introduction, 83
  fully satisfactory, 66
  for Horwichian concept of truth, 65,
    142n4
possession condition (PC*)
  in AHM, 71–4
  difference from possession condition
    (PC), 71
  Peacocke's theory about, 94–6, 101
possibilities
  commitment to existence of, 42
Prior, A. N., 27, 135n18
property-exemplifications
  as states of affairs, 42
  as terms of singular causation, 42
propositional variables
  binding, 20, 132n8
  devices playing same role as, 26–7
propositions
  absolute, 62–4
  absolute and relational, 61–3, 70–4

beliefs independent of empirical
  evidence, 14
containing nondesignating singular
  concepts, 113, 115
eternal, 67
as exceptions to bivalence, 113–14
logical structures of, 2–3
with normative concepts, 113–15
relational, 61–2
that apply vague concepts, 114
use of term, 1, 2–3
*See also* thoughts; truth, propositional
Putnam, Hilary, 28–9, 32, 97, 135n19

quantifiers
  existential substitutional, 18
  objectual, 18–19, 132n8
  substitutional, 18
  universal substitutional, 18
  *See also* substitutional quantification;
    substitutional quantifiers
Quine, W. V., 5, 24, 32, 89, 128n6,
  130n3, 134n13
Quirk, Randolph, 143n8

Ramsey, F. P., 5, 128n6
reference
  account provided by simple
    substitution, 29–30
  definition of, 38
  distinction between two forms of,
    130n20
  internal connection between
    causation and, 28–30
  as relational semantic concept, 7
reliability
  of deductive inference, 103–5
  definable in terms of truth, 91–2
  of inductive inference, 104–5
  principle, 91–2

reliable indication, 7, 91, 103–4

representations

determinate and determinable,
59–61, 87

eternal, 64–5, 67

representations, indexical

minimalism to explain semantic
properties of, 64

as problem for deflationism, 58–9

relationships between contexts and,
61

semantic propositions concerned
with, 70

Ross, W. D., 128n7

Russell, Bertrand, 6, 130n16

Salmon, Nathan, 127n2

satisfaction

formal definitions of concept of, 88

Tarski's notion of, 87

SEM. *See* simple extended minimalism
(SEM)

semantic concepts

explained by substitutional
quantification, 23

objections to simple
substitutionalism based on, 28–30

semantic concepts, relational, 7–8, 94

contribution to knowledge, 90

explanation for possession of, 106–7

theoretical utility of, 106

utility of, 89–91

value of, 94

semantic correspondence

definition of, 49

in extended substitutionalism, 56–7

intuitive relation of, 49–50

principle of success, 105

salience of, 50, 106

semantic notions

AHM as guide in theory of, 70

semantic properties

of inaccessible thoughts, 79

semantic relations

folk psychology principles about
(12–18), 101–6

simple extended minimalism (SEM), 70

AHM proposition entailed in, 72–3

consequence running counter to
intuitions, 72

counterpart of principle (G), 71–2

differences from AHM, 70

liberalization of account of, 75

in relation to indexical thoughts,
72–3

revision to meet problem of
intercontextual knowledge, 75–6

skepticism

about semantic properties of
concepts and thoughts, 15–16,
23, 130n3

Quinian, 130n3

Soames, Scott, 127n2, 143n11, 146n5

sortal concept, 98

states of affairs

actuality as property of, 51

actuality–neutral concepts of, 46

canonical names for, 46–8

causes and effects as, 44

commitments concerning actuality
of, 46

commitments to, 42, 45

in correspondence intuitions, 41–6

existence as property of, 51

in extended substitutionalism, 56

possible, 41–2

property-exemplifications as, 42

propositions as, 3

relation to thoughts, 49
world composed of, 45
Strawson, P. F., 5, 128n6
substitutionalism
  claims about concept of truth, 83
  commitment to incoherence thesis,
    118–19
  endorses intuitions favoring
    bivalence law, 114–15
substitutionalism, extended
  claims about truth conditions, 85–6
  claims of, 56
  as compromise between deflationism
    and correspondence theory,
    56–7
  function of, 56
  in grasping inaccessible thoughts, 85
  semantic correspondence
    acknowledged by, 56–7
  semantic correspondence of, 56–7
substitutionalism, simple
  as alternative version of deflationism,
    10
  claims of, 22–3
  meshes with Quinean explanation of
    utility of truth, 24, 134–5n15
  objection derived from reference and
    semantic concepts, 28–30
  power of, 22–3
substitutional quantification
  as analytic tool of simple
    substitutionalism, 32
  contribution to expression of
    generality, 134n15
  defined, 17–22
  paradoxical nature of, 121–6
  possession condition for existential,
    83–4
  role in thought and discourse, 24–7

semantic concepts explained by, 23
truth in terms of, 17, 84
substitutional quantifiers
  binding nominal variables, 132n8
  binding propositional variables, 20,
    132n8
  binding variables appropriate to
    singular concepts, 23
  binding variables appropriate to
    whole thoughts, 23
  Existential Elimination rule, 19–20,
    118, 125
  Existential Introduction rule, 19, 83,
    117–18, 125
  paradoxical nature of, 121–6
  Universal Elimination rule, 18, 117
  Universal Introduction rule, 19, 117

Tarski, Alfred, 6, 87–8, 119, 129n15,
  146n3
Tarski's theory of truth, 86–8, 129n15
Taylor, Ken, 129n15, 143n11
thoughts
  accessible and inaccessible, 71–3, 75,
    77–82
  determinable and determinate, 59
  eternal, 64–5, 73
  expressed by nonlinguistic behavior,
    78–9
  good translations of inaccessible,
    79–80
  have truth conditions, 85–6, 115
  indexical, 58, 73, 87
  interpretive counterparts of, 78–9
  normative, 54
  relation to states of affairs, 49
  relevant notion of good translation
    of, 76–7
  truth conditions of, 85–6, 115–16

thoughts (*cont.*)

   truth values of, 80

   use of term, 1–2, 3

truth

   Aquinas's definition of, 6

   Aristotle's definition of, 5

   Avicennna's definition of, 6

   correspondence theory of, 6, 39,
      54–5

   defined by SEM, 71

   deflationism as theory of, 3–4, 6

   doxastic, 2

   extended Horwichian account of, 82

   Horwich's theory of, 4, 11, 39, 64–6

   intuitions about, 39, 119

   ordinary concept of, 87

   Plato's account of, 128n9

   a priori propositions involving
      concept of, 17

   Quine's theory of utility of, 24, 32,
      55, 89, 134–5n15

   relationship between actuality and,
      50–2

   SEM concept of, 71

   sentential, 2

   simple substitutional theory of, 22

   substitutional quantification in terms
      of, 17–18

   substitutional theory of, 112

   Tarskian concept of, 87–8, 129n15

truth, propositional

   concept of, 1–2

   Horwich's concept of, 4, 11

   sentential and doxastic truth in terms
      of, 2

truth concept

   applied to normative thoughts,
      54

   role in descriptive and explanatory
      practices, 24

truth conditions

   of accessible and inaccessible
      thoughts, 75–6

   claims of extended substitutionalism,
      85–6, 115–16

   classified as states of affairs, 116

   direct and indirect grasping of,
      75–6

   knowing by grasping, 116

   of a thought, 85–6, 115

truth theory

   deflationism as, 3–4

   simple substitutionalism, 22–4

Universal Elimination

   inferences involving, 20–1

   as rule of inference for substitutional
      quantifiers, 18–19, 117

Universal Introduction

   restrictions governing, 22

   as rule of inference for substitutional
      quantifiers, 19, 117

van Inwagen, Peter, 138n5

Van Riet, S., 129n10

Varzi, A., 137n2

William of Auvergne, 6, 129n11

Wittgenstein, Ludwig, 6, 27, 130n17,
      135n17, 137n4